patagonia® notes from the field

Edited by Nora Gallagher
Introduction by Yvon Chouinard

CHRONICLE BOOKS
SAN FRANCISCO

Page 1: Dave Seoane dropping in. Chamonix, France.

Facing title page: Cutting through the brash in the Beagle Channel, Tierra del Fuego.

Opposite: Hiking in winter on "the Racetrack," Death Valley.

This book was printed on a sheet-fed printing press, using soy-based four-color process inks. The paper stock used for the interior of the book consists of chlorine-free Japanese matte art paper. The case material is recycled chipboard.

The body text is set in Scala, and the captions and essay titles are in Scala Sans, both designed by Martin Majoor in 1990 and 1993, respectively.

© 1999 Patagonia, Inc.

Printed in Hong Kong.

Library of Congress Cataloging-in-Publication Data:

Patagonia : Notes from the field / edited by Nora Gallagher.
p. cm.
ISBN 0-8118-2604-x
1. Natural History. 2. Ecology. I. Gallagher, Nora, 1949-
QH81.P3428 1999
508—dc21   99-18491
                        CIP

Photo editor: Jennifer Ridgeway
Design: Shawn Hazen
Cover photograph: Didier Givois/ Adventure Photo

Distributed in Canada by
Raincoast Books
8680 Cambie Street
Vancouver, BC V6P 6M9

10 9 8 7 6 5 4 3 2 1

Chronicle Books
85 Second Street
San Francisco, CA 94105

www.chroniclebooks.com

Contents

Introduction

Sunset atop El Capitan, Yosemite.

LIKE MOST THINGS AT PATAGONIA, this book is rooted in the sport of climbing.

As much as anything else, climbing is about waiting. Waiting for the weather to clear. Waiting for the snow and ice to set. Bivouacking on a small ledge, waiting until it's light and we can start up again. And in all that waiting, there is storytelling.

I think back to 1968, my first trip to Patagonia. After making base camp at Fitzroy in November, four friends and I spent the next two months waiting—thirty-one of those days in ice caves. We told a lot of stories waiting out the incessant storms.

Thirty years later, this experience is not uncommon in Patagonia. One of our employees, Mikio Suizu from our Majiro store in Tokyo, recently made seven attempts of Cerro Torre over a period of three months. Despite his long wait, he never had a break in the weather long enough to allow for an ascent. He finally quit when his ice cave opened into a yawning crevasse and swallowed all of his gear. Mikio returned with a lot of stories and a better command of English and Spanish.

I've always chosen my climbing partners carefully, but in that two-month wait at Fitzroy, I learned that someone's value to an expedition could largely be determined by their storytelling skills. Lingering on the details of distant events, describing and interpreting the natural setting, waiting as long as possible before saying the obvious—these skills are not frivolous. They delay the onset of insanity. They help stave off boredom. And boredom is what causes climbers to move on, to start climbing when it simply doesn't make sense to do so. Imagine that: storytelling to save lives.

The stakes aren't often as high in the other nature-oriented sports, but storytelling is still part of the culture. Waiting for the right surf conditions can take time, and if the waves aren't breaking, there is no surf. The waits are usually shorter than on a mountain—sometimes it's for the tide to come back in or for the wind to change direction. But the "you should have seen this place yesterday" stories only last so long, and so the waiting is filled with other stories.

I've often felt lucky that I've been active in outdoor sports at a time when so much about them was new. I was white-water paddling when it seemed nearly every river had never been run. I was surfing at Malibu when you wished another surfer would show up to share the waves with you. And climbing in the Big Wall era, our summers were marked by a string of first ascents. When each of these sports was in its formative stage—and before formal competitions were introduced—discussions often took on an ethical tone. What relationship should a climber have with the rock? What reductions in risk are acceptable and which ones change the sport utterly?

The tone of these discussions was reflected in, and shaped by, the 1972 Chouinard Equipment catalog (Chouinard Equipment was a predecessor of Patagonia). We led with an essay that raised ethical questions about the way we climbed—and in the process, we changed the sport utterly. Over a span of fourteen pages (we somehow found room to squeeze in products on the remaining pages), Doug Robinson outlined the need to move away from the use of pitons.

There is a word for it, and the word is clean. Climbing with only nuts and runners for protection is clean climbing. Clean because the rock is left unaltered by the passing climber. Clean because nothing is hammered into the rock and then hammered back out, leaving the rock scarred and the next climber's experience less natural. Clean because the climber's protection leaves little trace of his ascension. Clean is climbing the rock without changing it; a step closer to organic climbing for the natural man.

Not your typical sales brochure.

And then there is what happens when one is not waiting, when one is moving along at a pace that allows for observation. No electronic media and no distractions—just the natural setting and the people with whom that place is shared. I remember a climb that T. M. Herbert and I did on El Capitan. By the seventh day of living on the wall, we now felt at home. Bivouacking in hammocks was completely natural. Nothing felt strange about our vertical world. With more receptive senses we now appreciated everything around us. Each individual crystal in the granite stood out in bold relief. The varied shapes of the clouds never ceased to attract our attention. For the first time, we noticed tiny bugs that were all over the walls, so tiny they were barely noticeable. While belaying, I stared at one for fifteen minutes, watching him move and admiring his brilliant red color. After a period of time—and you can't speed this up—the artist gets caught up in the sculpture, and the material comes alive. That was happening to both of us at the same time, and as we talked aloud about it, our powers of observation grew even stronger. How could one ever be bored with so many good things to see and feel! This unity with our surroundings, this ultra-penetrating perception, gave us a feeling of contentment we had not had in years.

The deliberate and painstaking pace of travel in climbing and mountaineering is remarkable. All travel was once this way, with traveling in fact more important than the destination itself. Now it's the opposite, because travel, really, has been eliminated: We get on a plane, and then we're there. But in climbing, the pace still allows for observation and for interpretation.

All of this—the storytelling, the ethical discussions, the pure observation—has shaped Patagonia and our catalogs over the years. It has enabled us to have a genuine dialogue with our customers. And because the quality of dialogue matters to us (again, going back to the notion that the quality of one's storytelling aids an expedition), we've found ways to make it an important part of our business. With that first essay by Doug Robinson, we found that we didn't need to settle for doing only what we needed to do, which was to describe our products. We proved to ourselves that we could also do what we wanted to do, which was to challenge our audience's imagination, engage them in discussions and with stories, and lure them into the outdoors and into environmentalism. We've ignored the sales-per-square-inch rule of catalog management—really, that's how it's taught in business school—and have focused instead on our relationship with nature and with our customers.

Sometimes this dialogue isn't easy. When our reputation for being a green business grew, we offered a bit of reality, opening one catalog with the statement that "Everything we make pollutes. Period." That started a healthy, and sometimes troubling, discussion among our readers; several years and thousands of letters and E-mails later, it's still going. Sometimes the dialogue borders on the frivolous. In the early 1980s, we found it necessary to explain why we shifted an entire industry away from making clothes only in shades of tan and green and toward colors like fushcia, cobalt, and French red. The essay quoted from the private letters of Flaubert.

In 1990, we stepped beyond the ethical discussions and began running field reports in each catalog. These observations on moments in nature were designed to reconnect with the climber's pace, to help our readers and ourselves hone our powers of observation, to keep alive the art of storytelling in nature. As we did so, we learned once again that descriptions can be as powerful as commands, and that people who take the time to see and learn from their time in nature can become effective activists in its defense.

We think we've hit on a good mix with our catalogs—one that just might stave off insanity after several weeks in an ice cave. Ethical discussions, often started with honest statements about the impact we ourselves have on the earth. Stories that are reflective, descriptive, or humorous. And the occasional basic adrenaline rush. That mix is reflected in this book.

The mix is also enhanced, as our catalogs always are, with photographs. In fact, most people who attempt to describe a Patagonia catalog start with the photographs. Brilliant clarity and color. Full-page images conveying a boundless sense of nature and adventure. Details emerging slowly, human activity not always evident at first glance. Humans in their place and in context—never on top and never dominating, just there as part of the scene. That scale is most often what makes them breathtaking—a small detail in the face of immense nature. In this book, we've not attempted to match the photos with the essays. My sense is that good writing doesn't require illustration. And these photos can stand alone, perhaps enhancing your own sense of observation.

This book is a collection of some of the best field reports to run in the Patagonia catalog—though at least a third of them have not been previously published. My hope is that as you read them you'll do what T. M. Herbert and I did on El Cap—you'll start to see things you've never seen before. And I'm also hopeful that these stories might move you to action.

Essays

Carlos Andrade

On Board *Hōkūle'a:* Aotearoa to Tongatapu

OUR NAVIGATOR HAS TOLD US that we should see land sometime this morning. No compass, sextant, or any other kind of instrument has been used on this thousand-mile passage from Aotearoa, the "Land of the Long White Cloud," to the only surviving independent Polynesian kingdom, Tonga. The first four and a half days were crisp, cold, and clear. Well-defined swell trains born in Antarctic waters accompanied us, along with pelagic albatross and shearwater.

We left Waitangi to follow the ocean highways of our Polynesian ancestors and reestablish contact with our far-flung cousins. The stars, wind, and swells speak to our navigators, who are the eyes of the *wa'a.* We, the crew, are the hands and sinews that move the wings to catch the lift and skim on the skin of the sea. On this, our ninth day, we have been through four and a half days of roiling clouds, whistling wind, and mountainous seas that have charged at us from two quarters, drenching the steersmen, navigator, and everyone else on deck. Below the flimsy canvas shelter the rest of the crew try to rest, but as our Tongan crewman says, "Inside same wet as outside!"

Two days into this storm, during the midnight to four A.M. watch, as the *wa'a* sizzled through dark rain under storm sails, lines of squalls began buffeting us. Suddenly, Mau Piailug emerged from his sleeping place under the tarp. Mau is a master navigator from Satawal in the Caroline Islands of Micronesia who learned navigation from his grandfather. During this voyage, he has acted as mentor to Na'inoa, our young Hawai'ian navigator, but has stayed in the background, never saying much, allowing Na'inoa to practice his newly acquired skills. However, on this occasion, he quickly ordered the crew on watch to take down all of the sails immediately.

The crew members obeyed without question, but they wondered what had prompted Mau to take command of the situation. For most of the voyage, he had only emerged for meals and to look at the sunrises and sunsets to gauge the weather; nothing seemed out of the ordinary at this time. The crew were looking at each other questioningly, when suddenly, gusts of wind in the 40 to 50 MPH range blasted the *wa'a.* The wind lasted about twenty minutes. If the sails had been up, much damage would have been done, and we might even have capsized. Mau told them to put the sails back up and went back to bed.

Some say that Mau's many nights at sea have made his senses so acute that he can feel the wind coming. Mau says that on his island the consummate navigator knows the ways of the sea and is a father to his crew, and also that he possesses magic.

Now we strain to see in the little light left by stars that intermittently show

Above: Cruising the highway to Tongatapu.

Opposite: The Hōkūle'a fishing for land.

Previous page: Avalanche on the west face of Dhaulagiri, Nepal.

themselves through the storm clouds. Orion died long hours ago in the west. The three stars in the handle of the Dipper stand vertically, beckoning like a bird's wing above the northern horizon. The Southern Cross sinks into the south as we plunge through the predawn. Naʻinoa tells us to look for land. There! Sione, our Tongan crew member, sees what he says is land. Forty-five minutes later, the rest of us finally see something. A darker shadow solidifies on the horizon right where he has been pointing, as the sun climbs up the back of the easterly winds. Low, ringed by coral fingers that reach out miles into the surrounding ocean, Tongatapu, "Sacred Tonga," spouts white with blowholes carved into her flanks by the ceaseless pummeling of the sea. At first we mistake the fountains of white for whales, then we laugh with relief knowing that dry beds and hot meals await us when we land. The navigator can rest now. Like Maui with his mighty hook, he has fished the land from the sea. He has raised the island.

Little Wild Places

AFTER GRADUATING from an inner-city high school twenty-some years ago, I had an epiphany of sorts as a hood-in-the-woods (as we were known then) on an Outward Bound course. In the exciting, stripped-down version of life on that trip, I was inspired to get the hell out of what seemed a dead-end life in Denver and spend my days in clean, crystalline, uncluttered, wild places. So far I have been very lucky to be able to keep that vow. Today, I work for an organization in northern New Mexico, the land of my three-hundred-year-old family roots, that advocates on behalf of wild, free-flowing, clean rivers and the traditional rural lifestyle that has developed along those rivers over the centuries.

There have been times since my escape that, like an overzealous convert to a new religion, I bad-rapped all things urban. But if working on environmental issues teaches anything, it is the undeniable maxim, cliché as it sometimes sounds, that all things are connected. "When we try to pick out anything by itself, we find it hitched to everything else in the universe," said John Muir. Pour your urban sewage into the river and it flows downstream and into a section of "wild" river you might want to float someday. Spew your electricity-producing coal smoke into the air and it obscures the view of the Grand Canyon next time you take your family there on vacation. And it flows both ways. The heavy-metal toxicity seeping out of the Molycorp molybdenum mine just up the road from where I live (one consequence of the lightweight mountain bikes we all like to ride nowadays) flows downstream toward drinking-water supplies for hundreds of thousands of people in Santa Fe and Albuquerque.

The barrier some people see between urban and rural issues, urban and rural lifestyles, is artificial. We can no longer hide from what lies upwind, upstream, or lurks somewhere in the food chain.

As the urban/rural boundary has blurred over the years, I've come to see that growing up in the city had its rewards. The inner-city life has adventures all its own, but I was also lucky to grow up in the city when I did, when there was still some open space around—untended little wild spots, overgrown orchards, vast open fields that seemed to stretch forever without a building, dense arbors in urban parks where we could hide securely from school and cops. We even used to swim without fear in urban lakes or in the abandoned gravel pit down the road that had filled with water. Maybe it was just the innocence and faith of youth, but I think the water was relatively clean back then. There were outdoor adventures— little and urban, but adventures nonetheless—to be had around every corner.

One cold, snowy day my friends and I chose to stay out and confront the elements rather than school. We found ourselves huddling in a cave formed by the

snow-laden limbs of an overhanging pine tree in the park. We were fifty feet from a busy street, the public library was a stone's throw in the other direction, yet we managed to turn the day into a wilderness survival epic. Poorly prepared for the wintry outdoors in our thin cotton Army-surplus jackets, but with plenty of matches for cigarettes (and other things), we gathered up enough dry wood for a small fire. We passed the entire day hunkered like feral humans around the fire, feeling the solid satisfaction of having come to terms with the elements and, I've always thought, each of us imagining ourselves around a campfire of yore in another time out on some remote frontier.

A rudimentary sense of connection with the big wild earth crept into my awareness with this and other experiences: catching crappies, frogs, and crawdads at nearby lakes; exploring the mysterious complexity of life at the wetland fringes; finding shelter among the overgrown vegetation of the old orphanage down the street. That such discoveries take place even in an urban environment gives me heart, and it becomes obvious to me that exploring our place in the natural world must be an extremely powerful and essential human instinct.

These experiences were the seeds of a relationship to the natural world that began flourishing when I first went into the woods. And I've come to realize, all these years later, that they are the seeds of inspiration for the work I do to protect wild places.

Wallace Stegner talked about a "geography of hope" as wild places—out there somewhere—that we might never even get to see. Those places are important for their own sake, if not for ours, but we also need that sort of hope closer to home, accessible to every kid growing up in the city today. Some of us are lucky enough to live in beautiful rural communities or have the means and the time to get to remote wild places and feel connected to the natural world. But even those of us fated by circumstance or economy to cramped urban neighborhoods have a basic right to this quality in our lives.

We can feel a true sense of hope when we all have little wild places to go to, where the earth still works its magic, where we can rekindle our fundamental relationship with the natural world.

Colorado river system.

The Question

FOR ABOUT TEN YEARS I would wake up almost every morning wondering whether I was taking the right course: abandoning the joy of fiction and the raw freedom of never knowing what each day would bring—never knowing the turns a story would take and, in fact, following most stories in the direction opposite where I might ordinarily have expected them to wander. I had instead launched myself—carelessly, recklessly, wantonly, daily—into advocacy on behalf of a small wild valley, the Yaak. Back then I was strong and young and never dreamed that strength, energy, or endurance might someday be available in anything less than an infinite supply.

The Yaak snugs right up against Idaho, and snugs up against Canada, too. It is both a pipeline to and a reservoir of wildness. It is both cornerstone and conduit. It's the wildest and most diverse valley I've ever seen in the Lower 48, with grizzlies prowling around in the forests down to elevations as low as two thousand feet as well as lynx, wolverines, wolves, sturgeon in the Kootenai River, great gray owls, bull trout, eagles, and on and on. And still, despite this wildness, there is not one single acre of protected wilderness in the half-million-acre valley.

The question I used to ask myself every morning was a simple question, one to which—each morning—I had only to answer yes or no.

Would this ravaged valley, which has been clear-cut to hell and back—only a tattered archipelago of roadless cores remains intact—be better off without my voice in almost every regard save that of my own conscience? The current, if not future, human community of shy hermits and government loathers might be more at ease were the plight of this valley's roadless lands still a secret. The present grizzly bear community (which at that point had dwindled to one remaining breeding-age female; now there are three) might be better off in the next few coming years if I'd just lay low and be quiet. The old ways of road building and clear-cutting are maybe, perhaps, just about gone, or surely soon to be gone, aren't they? (Though ten years ago, they were not just about gone.)

It's true that the Yaak has been hacked hard, but maybe that's all over. Wasn't there a chance that without even having to say anything, or advocate for anything, things would just stay the way they are, which is pretty much the way all of us up here—myself included—want them to stay? That's the question.

I didn't hear many other voices speaking out on behalf of the Yaak's roadless cores, either in the community or in the larger, more empowered world. So I started asking for help. I made my decision, even though I suspected the news of yet another significant place in peril might bring onlookers whose ephemeral visits could occasionally, like a brief rainstorm, compromise the peace of hermits

Biologist Karen McAllister searching the Waump River, British Columbia.

such as myself, and the grizzlies, the wolves. (There aren't many trails in the Yaak, and fewer vistas; as far as human recreation goes, a beer at the tavern and a beer at the Dirty Shame about covers it.) Still . . . *tourists*, or, as my three-year-old daughter pronounces the word, *terrorists*.

It's not a beautiful valley, really, to visitors: It's dark and rainy and snowy and spooky. (This year, we've had only four days of sunshine out of the last hundred.) Unlike most places in the world, this is a great place to live, but not much to visit. My worst fear, nonetheless, is of a wave of yuppie acquisition—of this ragged but rich landscape somehow becoming infected with the gnawing, consuming contagion that's spread throughout the West, in which industrial recreationists look at a landscape and think not, "What can I do to help keep this place the way it is," but rather, "What's in it for me?"

In conjunction with a group of friends up here, I've been working my ass off for the last half-year trying to get some small timber sales of dead and dying trees conducted from existing road systems set aside for the handful of loggers who still live in the valley, and to give the local small mill owners first right of refusal on those logs.

It won't change the world, if we're successful. It won't save that culture. But it will buy time, which is almost the same thing. Nothing lasts forever.

The woodworkers are scared to death of me. They think my desires for protected wilderness areas in the last roadless cores would only be the beginning. They believe that the government would then begin evicting them from house and home, devouring the entire community as the old clear-cutters once devoured whole mountains up here.

So I'm caught now between two worlds, just as I was once caught between fiction and advocacy: working for the last few bands of independent loggers and mill owners, and working, as ever, for the little unprotected wilderness that still remains. Moving back and forth, here and there, in the worst combination of both restlessness and weariness.

What I like about the notion of wilderness designation is that I could stop fighting, year after year, on behalf of roadless areas. I could go back to my other life—if it still waits there for me. I don't think backpackers would flock to the Yaak. It's not like the rest of the West. It's a swamp—a biological wilderness, not a recreational wilderness.

If it's like this for me, in my soft, privileged life—stressed between the two sides of a question, and the two lives—what must it be like for the grizzlies and wolves?

I haven't even thought about the question—to be quiet, or to work for what I believe in and need—in over two years.

A young woman who had the great fortune to have been born here, and to grow up here, once asked me the question. She was understandably upset that I'd said the secret name of her home, my home, to the larger world—the name of this valley. She wanted to believe, I think, that things would stay the same, and that voicelessness, not voice, was more honorable as well as prudent.

She didn't agree with the abuses of the past either, but wanted silence, just a little more silence, in the moment. I guess she assumed the future would take care of itself, or that the future turnings of the outside world would avoid the valley, or maybe even take care of things on the valley's behalf.

And maybe they will. But it has not been that way here in the past. My experience has been that the future devours. It does not protect.

This is not a place to come to, but it is a place to protect.

I would still like to know that these last roadless cores can be put out of harm's way forever.

As soon as that's achieved (in the Yaak, conservationists have been trying, unsuccessfully, for thirty-five years now), I'll get real, real quiet.

I'll walk into the dark woods and sit down.

I don't know what I'll feel. But I know that day will come. I just know it.

Who you can write to, and what you can say:

Please keep the last remaining roadless lands in the Yaak Valley as they are, roadless, forever, with a wilderness designation.

Mike Dombeck,
Chief of U.S. Forest Service
Box 96090
Washington, D.C. 20090

Governor Marc Racicot
State Capitol
Helena, MT 59620

Supervisor
Kootenai National Forest
Highway 2 West
Libby, MT 59923

Dave Bean

The Fall

GROWING UP, everyone takes something of their childhood with them, as if to stave off that inevitable loss of innocence. I took my bicycle on the road out of adolescence toward adulthood. Falling down a slickrock desert cliff stopped me from thinking like a teenager. I was thirty-two.

I bike the eighteen-inch-wide section of the Poison Spider Trail called the Catwalk, a fantastically dangerous route with a sandstone cliff falling away hundreds of feet on one side. Entering the Catwalk I actually believe my balance to be highly evolved.

Before this day I thought mountain bikes were manifest destiny. Once, racing friends down a two-track, I looked back to gauge my lead and when I faced forward again I stared at a Jeep's front grille. I slid my bike sideways beneath the Jeep, kicking free at the last moment.

On the Catwalk I feel the pressure of my right pedal against an object, a skull-size rock that levers my machine, my feet still clipped in. I'm going over and already it's too late to turn against it. In that gaping moment of lost balance I become keenly observant. I see that the cliff slopes at a sixty-degree pitch—all shale, sand, and loose stone—before the rock cuts back on itself in a fatal vertical face. I was brought up to believe that each of us controls our own destiny, but as I go over, the wind whistles through my ears like a hawk scream and I know I've been handed a line.

My body hurls sideward through space. My life refuses to flash before my eyes like a music video; the one I love never appears in a vision; and I don't forgive my seventh-grade English teacher for making me feel hopeless. Three seconds feel like an eternity. I think of how little I understand about mountain bikes, gravity, or the surreal edge of the desert, and how, out of everyone I know, I least deserve to die.

In the air I try to grab my bike. It is worth almost one thousand dollars. The thing about falling is that I can watch myself as I go, even upside-down turning flips. By this time I'm tumbling closer and closer to that fatal drop. Beyond it is nothing but air. I can't seem to arrest myself. Then suddenly I catch. My bike flips to the cliff edge and stops. The front wheel spins free over the abyss.

For a while my wife bugged me to get a new rear wheel because of a flat spot that goes thump da thump. But I like the bumpy feel when I occasionally bike. It reminds me of how arrogant and selfish I was to imagine that I might cheat gravity, the desert, or adulthood.

Cooking in Hell's Kitchen

AS THE SUN DROPPED behind the jagged horizon, Hell's Kitchen Canyon, in the northern Wasatch of Utah, cooled down quickly. We retreated past our snowboards that bristled around the yurt's entrance like a formidable fence swaying in the evening breeze.

The outside temperatures spiraled to almost zero, but inside our little illuminated canvas cone it was tropical. I sweated, even took off my socks, while our guide, Ken, whipped up backcountry pesto pasta and French bread, and urged all of us to go out and pay homage to the end of the day. "Never know if it'll come up tomorrow," he winked. So Matty, Jason, Andy, Justin, and I ducked out in bootliner slippers for a sky show of colors—pink to rose to red to an eventual green moon rising behind a wall of aspens amid the pyramid peaks that surrounded our camp.

The moon was full, like our plates, and between mouthfuls we contemplated lines already claimed by Andy and Jason for the next morning. These would be pioneering descents, as we were the first snowboarders to slog up Hell's Kitchen Canyon, according to Ken, who broke trail on telemark skis, carried the heaviest pack—climbing vertical feet like a Sherpa at sea level—and seemed stoked beyond belief to be sharing his yurt with a bunch of twentysomethings. "Makes me feel young. When I was your age I . . ." Then the forty-eight-year-old Vietnam vet who was drafted in '67 talked to us about a war. "I used to carry a twenty-five-pound machine gun with forty-five pounds worth of ammo hanging from my pants, not

Above: Nightlife in the northern Wasatch.

Opposite: A shooting star on "Meteor at Sunrise." Chugach Mountains, Alaska.

to mention a flak jacket and helmet," he said, straddling a hatchet-scarred log next to the stove. "And I did not want to be there." A long pause followed as he sipped tea and shook his head at some long-buried memory. Then he smiled, a big red-bearded gentle grin, the type I might have expected from a pacifist in Canada in the '6os, not from a grunt. "This skiing, or snowboarding," he corrected himself, "is cake compared to that. I *want* to be here."

"Mail, that's what got me through. Ski magazines. Skiing. The snow." As he said *skiing*, he tapped his head and we all nodded and understood. "Thinking about skiing gave me hope over there. Doing those exercises—side steps and stuff in the jungle—kept me sane. My buddies thought I was a freak."

I went to sleep, staring into the embers that glowed red out of the woodstove, our gear hanging from hooks and lines above, casting long shadows upon the canvas walls. I heard choppers in my dreams and awoke to the hissing of a lantern and the smell of flapjacks on an iron griddle. I thought it was the middle of the night, but Ken was already geared up and grinning in the predawn hours as though he'd never slept. From my bunk, I watched him separate thick pieces of meat, and I asked him, "You sleep okay?" "Like a log," was his response. "Love it out here, the wind through these aspens." He held out a cup of coffee, but I declined, opting to poach his aura instead. As the others stirred, I pulled myself off the bunk and outside, where I watered a nearby tree in the crackling cold and caught whiffs of bacon frying, quite possibly the greatest smell on earth when it's winter and you're in back of beyond.

Suddenly hungry, I watched as the distant sunrise spilled over the tips of the highest peaks, painting the upper cornices, ridgelines, and couloirs we'd be riding in a few hours, and even though I was still dressed in long underwear and a T-shirt, I stood for some time (shivering) next to our snowboards, our weapons of choice for assaulting these mighty Wasatch peaks.

Finally, the bacon got the best of me, and I entered our bunker of good vibes, thankful that I have no idea what napalm in the morning smells like. Inside, Ken waved me to a seat with a spatula. "First chair, first tracks."

I decided right then that today's fresh tracks would go to Ken.

Tom Brokaw

The Do Boys Have Done It Again

Members of the Russian Far East Expedition.

WHAT THEY HAD DONE THIS TIME was to sweep me up into a dangerously over-loaded and well-worn Russian Aeroflot helicopter for a flight to an unknown destination in the Sikhote-Alin wilderness. Our guide was a Russian wildlife biologist we had met just twelve hours earlier, a muscular and noisy man of overflowing confidence and uncertain credentials. We bribed our way onto the flight with $280 American and a half carton of Marlboros; six of us with packs, kayaks, fly-fishing gear, and food, including enough olive oil and Parmesan to feed Sardinia for a winter.

The flight took us up the shoreline of the Russian Far East, a long, beautiful stretch of coastal cliffs and narrow beaches with little sign of settlements along the Sea of Japan.

We opened the chopper portholes for a better look and passed among us our lone aerial map of the peninsula. What the hell, I thought to myself, we may not know where we're going, but with the map we'll know where we are. We handed the treasured document to Doug Peacock, a Do Boy with the manners and movements of the grizzlies he's so skillfully studied. He took it in one paw and held it up to the porthole for a better look. Whoosh, it was gone, sucked out of the porthole and into the airstream. Tompkins and Chouinard smiled the secret smiles of those who like to see the stakes raised. All that was raised for me was my nausea level, but then, given Doug's record in these situations, I was grateful he hadn't lost my kayak.

Our final village stop came at dusk, and the helicopter crew scrambled to refuel and lift off for the lengthy and illegal detour we had purchased. They would fly four hours off their route before returning to their home port, Vladivostok, without fear of reprimand, since in the world of Aeroflot, four hours overdue is an on-time arrival.

Our new Russian friend, Dima the biologist, had insisted we explore the vast Bikin River watershed, the heart of the taiga, a two-million-square-mile expanse of temperate forest stretching west into Siberia. It's the home of the Siberian tiger, giant brown bear, moose, boar, and sable. It's unlikely any Westerner had penetrated the area of our destination.

Airborne, *wilderness* took on a new meaning. In every direction trees, rivers, gorges, mountains, and no sign of habitation. No roads, no cabins, no distant smoke or light. There was, however, one disturbing sign of intrusion: a scar of illegal clear-cutting by Hyundai, the South Korean conglomerate, which is moving on the timber with a rapacious appetite and, so far as we could tell, no consideration for native sensibilities or environmental preservation.

Aerial view of the shoreline. Russian
Far East.

It was at once exhilarating and, for me, a little unsettling. After all, I am accustomed to knowing exactly where I'll be every weeknight at exactly the same time. It may be the Saudi desert in predawn darkness or Red Square or Lhasa or Soweto, but it's 6:30 P.M. in New York and I'm on television. Now there I was in a Russian helicopter looking for a place to land in a trackless forest, and not even I knew where we were or where we would be two hours from now, much less tomorrow.

Dima promised two hundred miles of virgin rivers, never before kayaked. Well, how about a virgin kayaker? The only time I'd fully assembled my Feathercraft was in a suite at the San Francisco Four Seasons, with the instructional videotape running smoothly through the player and room service just two digits away.

Chouinard, Tompkins, Ridgeway, and Jib Ellison, our Russian-speaking California white-water artist, were on their feet as the big helicopter began to make tight, descending turns into a meadow above a free-flowing river. As it settled into the marshy grass, we were quick out the door with our gear. No turning back.

Now, just as I have you poised, prepared for the Russian version of *Heart of Darkness,* this welcome news: As I got my bearings, I could see to the side of the open meadow a tidy, one-room hunter's cabin. It was occupied, it turned out, by the master hunter of the region and his companions from the local tribe, the Udage. Dima, as it turned out, was the John Colter of the Russian Far East, known throughout the taiga for his woodsman's skills and voluble personality.

By darkness I had assembled my kayak, made a favorable assessment of the water, and sat fireside eating moose liver served up by our new friends. They, in turn, inhaled the fifth of scotch I had brought along as barter. It was a fair trade, and a fair evening breeze promised adventurous days ahead. The Do Boys had done it again. They had wrestled me away from the demons of my day job and set me free to float on the heady currents of the unknown.

Taming Gumbo

Laissez les bons temps rouler.

THEY CALL IT GUMBO, but it's nothing you'd care to eat. It's best described as a situation. A bad situation.

Color is the only resemblance this gumbo has to the belly-warming concoction laced with seafood and powdered sassafras popularized by southern Louisiana cooks. It's usually dark as the River Styx, but it can also be red, white, or gray, depending on local geology.

Gumbo is the boot-and-wheel-grabbing ooze created when a claylike soil absorbs just enough water to become, well, impassable. Found just about anywhere, gumbo usually lies between you and great fishing. Prolonged rain, a little flooding, or quick thaw are nature's favorite gumbo recipes.

Gumbo halts everything. Wheels lose traction. Boots are lost forever. The right mixture creates a perfect clinging ability that builds quickly to wedge tires against fenders. That's before you sink to the frame or windows. A suction grip is created. You must sell your soul to escape.

I smirk at the advertisements for the new generation of commuter-coveted "sport utility vehicles" blasting through rivers and screaming down nasty trails. I simply re-picture these handsome steeds of sweet-smelling leather, plush carpet, and exquisite trim packages buried to the headlights in the real world of gumbo. Gimme that rig and I'll show you places it can't go!

I still think about this delicious Western spring creek I'd lusted for years to prowl. When it changed hands I finally got permission. Several friends and I walked in. We needed CPR after we saw the size of the brown trout cruising and sipping. These tankers hadn't seen flies in our lifetime. What a day of fishing! Our backing knots got a workout. But everything has a price.

The ranch manager, a master irrigator with a reputation based on a love of greeting trespassers with the unforgettable sound of a 30-30 shell being jacked into his ancient Model 94, was friendly as can be. Late that afternoon he came by and drove me back to my 1971 Blazer. "Jest drive 'er right on down there and pick up your pals. You'll be fine," he grinned. I should have suspected something right then.

With the later afternoon sun blasting right in my face, I mistakenly tried to retrace his suggested path. The guy must have trained water to run uphill. He'd created a field so soft and gooey that no four-wheel drive could have crossed it without sinking. Yep. I found a gumbo patch and I was buried.

With nothing in sight to winch to, the best home remedy for vehicular gumbo extraction is the Handyman Jack. This indispensable tool of yesteryear was made by the Hi-Life Company in Bloomfield, Indiana. They're the best gumbo insurance

this side of a platinum AAA card. With thirty-seven inches of lift, I've used them to hoist equipment, rescue sunken boats, straighten jackknifed trailer tongues, truck bumpers, and frames as well as to change tires and add chains. My truck doesn't leave the garage without a Handyman.

This was a tedious process where inches counted. The jack would slowly and systematically raise one wheel at a time into view, allowing abandoned fence posts to be installed underneath. We had barely enough wood to make a short trail. I'd inch the rig ahead, dig up the old stuff, and repeat the jacking procedure. Long after total darkness and besieged by clouds of hungry mosquitoes that rose from the soggy field to devour us, we reached high ground. It must have taken forty-eight tries. Our hands, backs, and clothes were pinched, strained, and ruined, in that order.

It took another hour to knock the gumbo off the windshield, equipment, boots, and ourselves so we could travel. That Blazer splattered enough gumbo down the ranch road to plant a brand-new field. Once back on the highway, the remaining gumbo had the wheels so out of balance that I could barely make 25 MPH.

The day's fishing was nearly forgotten, but not quite. Everyone was too tired to talk. "You think that nice old guy set you up?" one friend asked.

"Yeah, I do," I ventured. "He's been guarding those fish for twenty-five years. I figure it was his way of letting the brown trout get a little revenge."

Fly-fishing in winter. Madison River, Montana.

Susie Caldwell

Five Water Stories

THE WOMAN ON THE FERRY put it best: "Everything in southeast Alaska is tied to the water. Your life is now tied to the water too."

1

I've come a long way on the back of a slow-moving ferry to land on a beach unlike any other surfacing in my waterlogged memory. Last night I was lulled to sleep by the ebbing tide, then awakened by its advancing flow with dreams of king salmon, starfish, and kelp rushing into the tent. This morning, in clumsy rubber boots, I shuffle along the kelp sidewalk looking for life.

I see starfish in colors stolen from a vegetable basket: beet starfish, squash starfish, eggplant starfish. They drape on one another like bloated relatives in a post–Thanksgiving dinner daze. I stop and listen to clam shells drag their heels as they're wrenched back to sea. I poke my finger into a gripping anemone fist, try to catch a sculpin, turn over a rock, and feel a worm slide from my hand back to the water. I look closer. These are not empty shells but hermit crabs, hiding in discarded snail homes, busy feeding on smaller naked sea creatures. I move on— step in—land a giant rubber boot in the shallow water. Listen to the dying screeches of barnacles.

2

Rain. I hear the barnacles inhaling the water, releasing their salt-soaked skin to the freshwater air. A thousand poppings and gaspings like heavy olive oil drops heating in a pan. I once read that the smell of rain is not the smell of rain at all, but the releasing of the earth's odorous chemical base. "When the barometric pressure drops, the soil exhales," the article said.

My friend who grew up on a farm insists that ripe cherries are the most delicate fruit in the world. "A single drop of rain can split a cherry in two," she told me. I didn't believe her. It's raining harder now. I think about putting on a jacket, but decide against it. My skin loosens and releases with each drop: I wonder how many it will take to split me in two.

3

I had forgotten that lakes are quiet waters. I am nestled on a fallen tree, one mile inland from the beach, an arm's length from where the horsetail-covered slope ends and this lake begins. There is no grinding of sand and stones, no broken shells. No sudden repeated crashings of water meeting shore, as if each wave were tripped from below. Just quiet water moving with the shifting wind. If I were

Perito Moreno Glacier, Argentina.

to go blind, how would I lead myself here? What is the smell of a lake born in a high mountain glacier? How does it taste when you sip gratefully from its banks?

4

Wake up still lost and thirsty on a steaming bed of moss. The mosquitoes have found me on this swamplike plateau Alaskans call a muskeg. It's time to move. Water oozes with each step, water too acidic to support much life. To survive here, you wait for a drop of rain and clutch it tightly—curling yourself inward like the leaves of the Labrador tea. To survive here, you change your eating habits, like the sundew.

I sink to my knees and examine this strange flower no bigger than my fingernail, a red carnivorous galaxy born in a bed of lichen. Then I see them—tiny insects caught between the folds of the sundew's pale skin—death in a drop of honey. I linger on my knees and watch the muskeg court the sun, unveiling its brilliant wheatgrass greens and raspberry reds in an otherwise skeletal landscape marked by windswept spruce and drowning lodgepole pines. Life here is older, more delicate than the rowdy world of tide pools. I peel off my noisy rain pants and think I am too loud, too awkward for the subtle, dangerous beauty of the muskeg.

5

It's early morning and this water looks cold. I kick off my running shoes, drape my clothes on the rocks, and sink my fingers into the gray-green water. Two bold steps and I would be deep enough to float on my back, deep enough to get my hair wet and say I swam in glacial waters. But for now, patting it with my hands feels brave enough. My earliest memory is of this gesture, patting the water in a big, blue, plastic basin.

I look up at the long blue tongue of Mendenhall Glacier and wade deeper in the river at its base. With numbing fingers, I jump up and throw the water high in the air. It falls on my back, my forehead, my neck. A geologist told me that a glacier's top layer is hard and susceptible to cracking, but the bottom layer is watery, flexible, pliable—a river awake under two thousand winter blankets. My body feels like the upper layer now. My skin winces and cracks, tries to push its way out of the frigid water. Then I remember what it's like, how good it feels to play in water, on water that moves, water that is still, that is frozen. Inside me, the waters are calm.

Of Avalanches and Weddings

Ice climber throwing rope to rappel.
Mount Temple, Banff National Park.

THALAY SAGAR IS AN ICE-PLASTERED GRANITE SPIRE in India. It had an obvious line that begged to be climbed, yet no team had ever attempted it. It was steep and the area was known for unstable weather, so the only way to climb was fast. Pretending to be bold, Andy and I waved good-bye to our pajama-clad cook and liaison officer, who was to be married in a couple of weeks. They were seriously playing cards.

After four days, three thousand feet of mixed rock and ice lay between us and the ground. At noon on the fifth day, we were following an intricate path of ice runnels and crack systems up this immense face when I felt a flake of snow hit my cheek. Within an hour, the rock holds and cracks were choked with fresh snow and a thick fog obscured the route. We were not in the ideal location to wait out a storm—the wall averaged seventy degrees and there were no flat places—but we had no choice. Andy prepared our anchors while I untangled the webbing used to suspend our port-a-ledge, a stretcher that hung from four straps off the anchors with a tentlike tarp for overhead shelter. There we were, perched at twenty-one thousand feet, nonchalantly setting aside food rations to hold us until the storm quit—four days, we thought, at the most. Outside, the snow fell harder.

Each day saw the same routine. Hot drink at 10 A.M., rest, half a cup of gorp at noon, rest, hot drink at 5 P.M., then sleep. At first the rest was welcome, but after two days, we were bored and spent most of our time entertaining each other with stories of epic climbs. On day four, the first avalanche began.

A wall of snow pounded against the fly and as I grabbed the webbing, I prayed that our shelter would withstand the force. Images of the poles collapsing and anchors pulling out of the rock sped through my mind. Then it was still. In fifteen minutes by my watch, another avalanche fell against the ledge. One after another, every fifteen minutes like clockwork.

"Man, I hope this doesn't last long," Andy sighed. We had an unspoken agreement never to express doubt, but desperation showed in his face, now gaunt and wrinkled. My stomach knotted tighter. Under the constant barrage of avalanches, retreat was impossible. We cowered in our bags as the storm swatted our ledge like a cat playing with a mouse. The avalanches went on for eight days.

At last the storm was spent. Humbled and starving, we began the retreat. In our weakened state, we only managed ten rappels on the first day. Then darkness caught us on an icy slope with insufficient anchors for the port-a-ledge. We hacked out a ledge in the snow-covered ice to sit on, and I pulled my sleeping bag up around my waist and held the stove in my lap as Andy tried to hold the tarp over us. Still snow managed to accumulate in my bag until it was so full I couldn't hold it up any longer. To calm myself, I thought of the feast our cook would prepare for us at base camp.

At first light, we started down again, and ten more rappels finally brought us to the base of the peak. My tension and fear were replaced by uncontrollable hunger. When we arrived at the camp, however, it was deserted. The wedding day had arrived and all that remained of our cook and liaison officer was a note and a deck of cards.

Kitty Calhoun leading on the north face
of Thalay Sagar.

Russell Chatham

One Salmon

WHEN THE GREAT RIVER SYSTEMS of western North America were created—the Fraser, the Skeena, the Columbia, the Sacramento, and the San Joaquin, to name only a few of the thousands—they were peopled with several kinds of salmon, fish of such grace, power, mystery, and pathos that some men have fallen in love with them as profoundly as with any woman.

In the northeastern corner of Nevada there is a stream called Salmon Creek. As recently as seventy years ago, maybe less, salmon came home here after a three-month journey from Astoria, up the Columbia and then the Snake River, to spawn and die in this peaceful, high-desert valley. When you walk along this stream today, there is an eerie feeling of loss, a loneliness and sorrow in its very gravels, like a mother mourning for an eternity over her dead children.

This stream is not alone in its grief. The sorrow extends to countless other childless mothers in California, Oregon, Idaho, Washington, and Canada, wailing a hopeless cry of longing across the continent for their doomed children, who can never, ever return because they are vanished forever from the face of the earth. In one recent year, a solitary sockeye salmon reached Idaho.

In the not-too-distant past when the salmon passed through the lower Columbia River they were so numerous as to be utterly uncountable. Sometimes individual fish were actually shouldered out onto the bank.

Recently, I stood on the ramparts of the Bonneville Dam, a site where once a trillion salmon swam by freely, and I knew then where the Devil himself lived, not in some imagined fiery cavern, but there inside the ice-cold concrete and steel. This was the epicenter of Hell, where Satan could murder the river and its children again and again, ruling an empire of satellite Hells, committing similar murder. The roar of the strangled water was like a raging howl of fear and loathing.

I was asked to join a committee and I did, knowing full well this was little more than waving a hanky in the face of tyrannosaurus rex. I considered explosives and legions of night soldiers, but this was clearly futile.

To neutralize the Devil requires an equal force, the force of God. But we are told He is not vengeful but rather, forgiving. He said vengeance is mine, but where is He when we need Him to lean over this part of the earth and unleash from His outstretched hand a torrent of fury and justice a hundred times the size of Krakatoa, the hydrogen bomb, and all the lightning bolts in history combined, setting off explosion after explosion, releasing vile gasses and clouds enough to darken the earth for a century, as the Devil's castles are blown to smithereens by deafening, blinding cataclysms at Oroville, Shasta, Hetch Hetchy, Nimbus, Dry Creek, Pillsbury, Grand Coulee, The Dalles, John Day, Bonneville, and a thousand other places? The Devil would return, as always, but at least it might take a while.

Chief Joseph Dam, Columbia River.

Greg Wilson catches some late season solitude. Big Wood River, Idaho.

Claire Chouinard

'Opihi Man

THE TROPICAL SKY WAS STAINED with blotches of darkening thunderclouds and a plume of smoke curled up from a bamboo structure at the end of the beach. Our group had paddled to this beach earlier in the day while the sun was still hot. My dad and I paddled in a plump, hot dog–shaped kayak. It was twenty feet long and inflatable. It caught the wind like a kite. I fought the water, and the wind. Every plunge of my paddle was like a blow to an enemy. As I stared ahead, I imagined my father doing the same behind me, squinting his eyes into the sun and wind. When he squinted, the creases around his eyes and across his tanned forehead became deeper and darker. But when I glanced over my shoulder, there was no strain in those eyes. He just casually dipped his paddle into the water and pulled. The muscles in his thick arms and shoulders shifted beneath his thin sleeves; I was reminded of the burning in my own forearms. It had been a long day and my stomach was starting to complain in a low voice.

We were now crouched like crabs on the rocks. The rocks just below the tide line were big and pink and smooth. They were only uncovered briefly as the ocean took a deep breath and pulled the waves back into its gut. During these seconds when the ocean seemed to part, we scampered forward with our bent knives to pry off the 'opihis. We had to be quick. If we were sloppy and had to try again we'd find their glossy orange lip sucked back under the dishlike shells. When they retracted they became impossible to dislodge. By the end of the afternoon our knuckles were bleeding and stiff from scraping rocks. The mesh dive bags secured around our waists began to sag and droop and catch between our legs. Finally finished, we began the trek back to our camp at the far end of the cove.

From a distance we could see the rest of the group huddled cooking in the shelter. Earlier, we had worked for hours digging through the rocks to clear a floor of flat hard sand. We had then bound bamboo poles together with strips of black inner-tube rubber and tied a blue tarp on as a roof. A few of the pieces of rubber were wrapped around knobs of lava that protruded from the mountain. They held the structure up and prevented it from catching the wind and blowing off the bank of the river.

My three aunties and I waded through the water, letting our bags hang in the current. The smell of buttery fried *moi* filled the air, and as we arrived the sight of glistening sashimi gave me a mouthwatering pang. I grabbed one of the slick slices of fish and let it slide down my throat. My stomach purred with relief. Keola and Jaya were slumped in the corner drinking amaretto from teacups and Dave was massaging Rell's neck. There was little talking as the four of us began placing our 'opihis on the grill. We cooked them with soy sauce, Hawai'ian salt, lemon,

Above: Lobsterfest, Christmas Island.

Opposite: 'Opihi at Sunset Beach, Hawai'i.

and hot pepper oil. They lay soft belly side to the sky with their own shells as little bowls. I had to look away when they poked their heads out.

"Claire, what is your father *doing*? Does he ever stop?" I looked from Rell's laughing smile to where my dad was climbing at the edge of the water. I couldn't see him from where I was sitting. He was blocked by the blue tarp. I looked back to the grill and watched the orange meat of the *'opihis* start to curl inward from the heat. I swayed slightly as I sipped my tea.

I didn't notice until I was alone in the shelter that everyone had moved. Even when Keola yelled to me that my father had fallen I didn't react. It couldn't be a big deal. Not until I saw him lying on his back curled inward in pain did I feel any fear. What was he doing? He looked like a little boy and then he looked like an ancient old man. He had been about fifteen feet up an overhang when the knob he was holding broke. The white spot where it had come loose glowed against the black lava. The bone from his elbow poked out and strained against his long white sleeve.

Rell and I used two pareus for a sling. He had lost the cap to his front tooth and hadn't shaved in six days. His face was shiny with sweat, and he cried out twice as we slowly helped him up through the rocks to the camp. I walked holding tightly to his good arm like I used to with my grandma in Chatsworth. He wouldn't let the boys carry him. While Glen radioed a friend who owned a helicopter, I watched my dad as if he were a television. He had his feet up on a cooler and a red sleeping bag up to his neck to prevent shock. It wasn't working very well.

His usually dark face looked like skim milk with a tint of blue under his eyes and on his lips. I was afraid to talk to him. He looked like I could hurt him. Something was missing from his face, or maybe something had been added. I didn't know this look. I didn't know those soft spots around his eyes. For the first time that evening I sat back on my heels and without shame let myself feel the exhaustion and tightness in my own arms and back.

I wasn't watching at first when his orange tan briefly returned. He opened his eyes and lifted half of his mouth into a grin.

"Hey, how're the *'opihis*?"

Bad Day at Flat Rock

Bob McTavish shaping.

SURFERS STILL TALK about the winter of '69 as having the best surf of the century in California. I was renting a beach cabin in the cove at Mondos and creating and forging climbers' equipment out of the old boiler room of the Hobson/Smith Packing Company.

Bob McTavish, the Australian surfer, was wintering in a cabin up the point and he and I spent a lot of time surfing together at the cobblestone point breaks of Ventura and Santa Barbara. Conditions there were ideal for perfecting his revolutionary wide, deep "V" short boards.

He mentioned one day that he wouldn't mind trying a bit of climbing, even though he admitted to not liking heights very much. In those days there were so few climbers that whenever we went climbing, we did new routes. For his introduction to rock climbing we knocked off a fine first ascent at Sespe, which is now called McTavish. The climb turned out to be more difficult than I had expected—especially the part going over the overhang and the vertical wall above. Bob remembers the day as a horrifying adventure, and he's never climbed again. I've always felt a bit guilty about the whole affair.

Twenty-four years later I'm at Bob's shop in Byron Bay in Queensland, and we two gray hairs are talking about having a surf together for old times' sake, even though we both know that the conditions are "victory at sea," with howling onshore wind and big wind waves. Bob knows a spot next to Flat Rock that might be more protected. On the way there he casually mentions that he has surfed this place fifty or eighty times and about 50 percent of those times he has seen a huge tiger shark that lives there but, "Don't worry mate, he's never bothered anyone yet."

Flat Rock is a reef that extends from shore and drops off suddenly in deeper water. With the waves so close together, the only way to get out is to go off the end of the reef, but with the medium high tide the rock is awash with white water from the waves crashing over the end. Bob waits for a lull, then runs and wades and jumps off the end—and just barely paddles over the next set, leaving me on the rock, gripping my surfboard with both arms to keep it from blowing away. I didn't mention I'd forgotten my wet suit, so all I had for protection was a rash guard.

I couldn't just chicken out, so off I go and near the end of the reef my right leg drops into a hole up to my crotch and gets stuck. Right away I remember the warnings I've heard about the blue-ringed octopi that live in these holes. One bite and you have mere seconds to live. I manage to get unstuck and I run back before the next wave crashes over. Now I'm really pumped, but I finally get outside and it's horrible. Just massive wind waves with no form sucking out over huge rock boils. As the adrenaline wears off I become aware that blood is pouring out of my leg and then my mind flashes on the shark. "Thanks Bob," I think. "We're even."

Michael Delp

Walking the River

I WALK UPSTREAM on one of those mornings when, if you look behind you, the rising sun is casting gold light into the trees. All the leaves are down and there is snow coming in from the west; the sky is an inky black. At thirty degrees, without the five layers that protect me I wouldn't last more than a few minutes before my body shut down. Upriver, in a shallow gravel run, old river browns are in the last sideways dances of their fall spawning. The river here is clear and cold. If you watch closely enough, you can see the slightest motions of their gills, how their mouths move up and down almost imperceptibly, their fins holding them in a perfect balance between water and sky.

Bring a trout out of the water and into the air and he suffocates. But underwater, in the cold, liquid atmosphere of a stream, his body moves the way the current moves. His skin ripples and gives against the current. A trout, bound only by the limits of its skeleton, the literal stretch of its skin, is close to being made of river.

Just before you release a fish from your hand, let your fingers slip down its sides while you hold it in the water. In that meeting of the two worlds, you above the waterline, the trout below, you are finally able to understand that the slightest pressure from the water means the slightest yield of its skin.

Back in the shallows the fish surge and slip sideways into each other. Egg and milt meet, then settle toward the safe harbor of the gravel below. All winter the trout grow into the river, the water moving over them, past them, through them.

I dip my hand into the water, holding it against the current. In less than a minute it goes numb. I leave it there as long as I can. Minutes later I'm dancing in front of the fireplace, my hand close to the flames, my skin coming back to life, the air of the room dense with the iron smell of the river running just below the window.

Looking for the last strike of the season.
Maroon Creek.

Daniel Duane

Fiji Evening

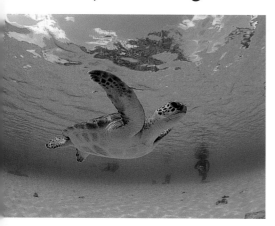

MOTORING OVER MOMI BAY, warm and wind-whipped below the storm-bound volcanic peaks of Viti Levu: sun nearing the horizon, surfers sitting dripping and smiling and holding the boat's gunwales, all of us halfway across the world to savor the rarest of treats. My own mind alive with the day's electric bluefish and cutting little shark fins, the varicolored coral that turns Antarctic energy into one of the greatest surfing waves on earth. Eyes still blinking from whites brighter than light, blues like a dream of the sea.

A turtle appears to starboard, ahead. Bobbing along in the adamantine ambient swell here inside the barrier reef, its path converges with our own. The boatman shouts in excitement and slows the engine to a crawl. We all tear through our packs, reaching for cameras. The boatman seems genuinely thrilled for us and he works to steady the boat, apparently wanting to give us an even platform. Then he cuts the engine altogether and we drift right toward the turtle.

"Ready!?" he cries out to us. Two guys from Hermosa Beach focus their wide-angle lenses. I turn on my Instamatic.

The boatman yells, "One! Two!"

The turtle reaches the side of the skiff, and the boatman barks, "Three!"

We snap our pictures, the turtle knocks into the bow and ducks under and disappears.

"What!?" the boatman cries out, apparently furious.

We're all confused.

"Why?" he says again.

"Why what?" I ask.

"Oh my God!" he shouts, looking at the sky in disgust. "What are you doing?"

We're not sure, really. Taking pictures?

In a silent fury, he yanks the engine on and plows into the hot darkness, gunning outraged U-turns, slamming into chop to bounce our fragile surfboards together and bruise our asses on the bench. And then, as the lights of the island grow near, I hear him. I hear him muttering to himself, "We should be having good dinner tonight . . . good dinner."

Above: Green turtle off Seven Mile Beach, Grand Cayman.

Opposite: Cloud Break, Fiji.

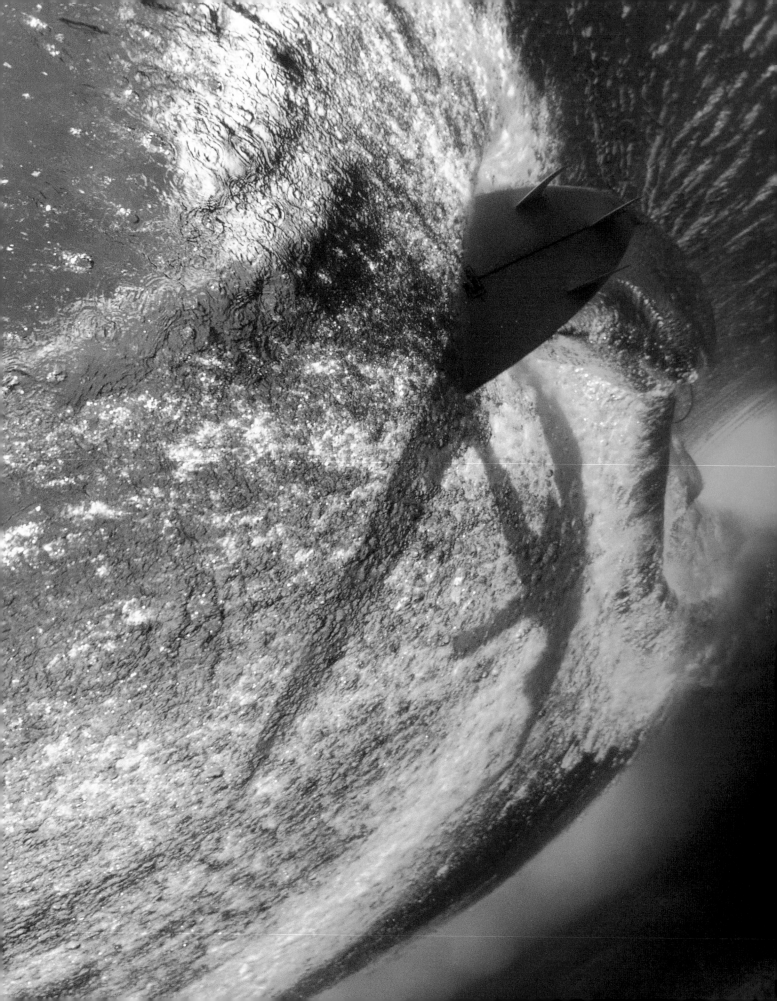

Ice Roses

On the day before Thanksgiving, six months after I'd moved to the banks of a Rocky Mountain trout stream, the temperature suddenly dropped fifty degrees. By the following week, the backyard trout stream I'd spent the whole summer fly-fishing had become a motionless, silent solid. The skies stayed clear and there'd been no snow all autumn, so each new stage of the freeze-up was perfectly visible.

On Day One, when the air hit zero, a viscous ice that looked like fog began to slide down the creek's clear current, sheathing everything in the stream—submerged trees, waterweeds, barbed wire, deer bones, car parts—in a soft cocoon of gray. On Thanksgiving proper, at minus five, I found myself standing like Saint Peter on pools in which just days before I'd battled brown trout. Day Three, minus eight, the glides froze over thick but clear as glass, and a prolific crop of geometric white roses sprang from that unlikely soil. I'd never seen such blossoms, or such terrain beneath. I'd stand in bright, heatless sunlight on what I still thought of as water, peering at white ice roses sprung from clearest glass, the fog streams and galactic currents of the creek flowing silent beneath the blossoms, the bottom stones glowing sunlit beneath the fog streams, and black, rose-shaped shadows dappling the glowing stones. On Day Four, even the fastest waters closed over and turned silent. The last little rapid became a heap of smashed china plates. Beavers slipped in and out of the broken china through small, carefully maintained holes. Stripped willow twigs piled like chopsticks at each hole.

The entire stream, turned solid, became my road into deep winter. I hiked it daily. And what these hikes reminded me of—no matter how cold the cold—was swimming through warm tropical reefs. Same complete immersion in intricacy and creativity. Same inexhaustible extravagance and style. Same inchoate gasps of thanks for all that I was seeing. Same no one listening, taking invisible bows.

Ice.

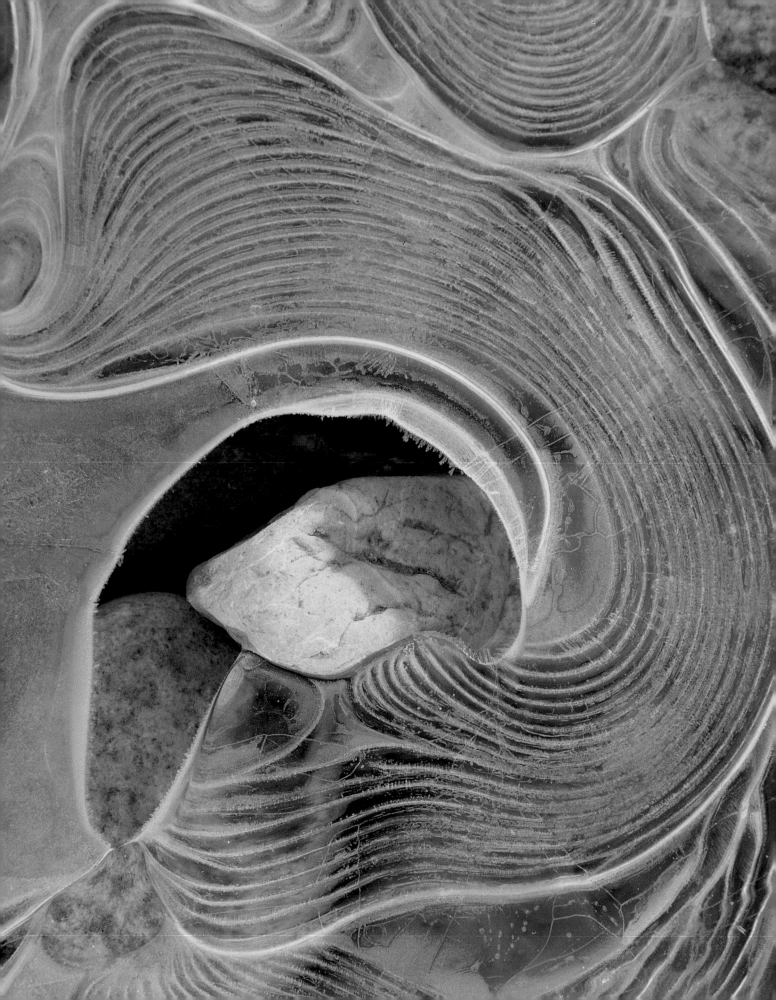

Two-person change, Moloka'i crossing.

John Dutton

Canoe Blessing

A THIN WOMAN in a simple flowered dress chants barefoot in the beach sand. She walks up one side of Holo Holo Waʻa, *our new outrigger canoe, and down the other, brushing the gunwales with dry grasses. A seabreeze rustles the palm fronds overhead and continues upcanyon to the spring-green Gaviota Coast hills.*

Out here, halfway between Catalina Island and Newport Beach, in late summer, things are far from serene. Six wooden paddles swing forward in unison, plant and drive the canoe forward through confused waters. Sweat runs in rivulets down straining backs, drying salt streaks shoulders. A sharp wind chop slaps the left quarter of *Holo Holo*, pushing against the *ama* and battling with the main hull. The *ama*, rigged on the left side of this forty-five-foot-long, two-foot-wide hull, is the float that provides essential stability. Without it, staying upright would be impossible. But as with most things, there is a downside. We're experiencing it.

The canoe is covered with flowers. Matched leis drape over the manu, *the upturned bow and stern. A string of flowers spirals down each* iaku, *the curved wooden beams that hold* ama *to hull. The flowers were carefully tended in a club member's greenhouse, hand-picked, sorted, and then threaded into leis one at a time. The woman brings salt water from the ocean in a koa wood bowl, mixes it with water carried from a nearby stream, and bathes the canoe in symbols both of its birth and its new home.*

As each wind swell in the channel hits the canoe, it catches the rear of our *ama*, pushing the stern right and kicking the bow left. The wave continues past the hull and a trough develops to our front right. Into that trough is where we want to go, surfing down swell, using the power of the ocean to push us faster than our paddles alone can carry us. Thus, the struggle that began two hours ago when we left the lee of Catalina. The *ama* pulls us left, we want to surf right.

Team members circle the canoe in silence to hear the prayer of blessing, and then lay hands gently on the boat, lift it off the cradles, and carry it to the water. It's only through the strength and coordination of these many hands that the four-hundred-pound canoe even makes it to the ocean.

The escort boat pulls ahead to drop the relief paddlers in our path as it has done regularly every fifteen minutes since the race began. These three paddlers combined with the six in the canoe make up our nine-man team. From the water they call out their seats: "Seat One!" "Seat Three!" "Seat Six!" We approach them on our left without slowing, two paddlers and myself, the steersman, roll out on the right side. The relief paddlers and a steersman haul themselves in on the left. Once again, refreshed muscle powers the canoe, and a refreshed steersman negotiates between wave and *ama*. Two wind swells build together on our left quarter, the *ama* kicks left as the swell passes, opening a trough to our right.

Cornwallis Island, Canada

I AM LYING ON A SLED on the frozen strait just off Cornwallis Island in the Canadian High Arctic. The sun is out; it's always out in May. I'm at the camp of an American seal biologist, Brendan Kelly. We have just been through a three-day storm that almost blew us away. Our water-closet tent vanished first, our food cache is buried deep, our insulated tent is leaning hard though the wind has now calmed. All that is left is ice and light. And with the one tiny notebook undamaged by drifting snow, I write:

> Light is a knife that cuts the edge of the polar continent.
> Where the ice shelf breaks off, what begins?
>
> Is ice a mirror?
> I walk.
>
> Light is a wall laid under me.
> I see you.
>
> Snow drifts in long
> rivers flowing from blocks of ice,
>
> the rivers drain:
> The floor of the world is blue.
>
> Ice is an eye.
> Eye is a heart.
>
> It sees that the body does not lie.
> It knows things.
>
> One day up here is six months long,
> followed by one night.
>
> Time takes two steps;
> light takes
>
> none at all.

Tiptoe through the ice floe. John Weld on Baffin Island.

Larry Elsner

Texas

FALL DAYS IN TEXAS can be scorchers. I forego synagogue on Yom Kippur in favor of the Hill Country landscape; shorts and hiking boots in place of suit and tie. I fast, out of tradition and a distorted sense of atonement, but allow myself trickles of water to quench my thirst. Just one of many rules I break on this most sacred of days. I've driven for nearly two hours, soothed by liturgical music courtesy of public radio, when I reach Enchanted Rock, a granite dome presiding over the greenery of Central Texas, to begin my annual trek. If I am lucky it is midweek, deserted, void of frolicking kids and panting parents. I pace myself, weakened by my fast. This is a day for reflection, and I hope to see my image in the occasional puddle, rainwater trapped in the concavity of the pink surface.

From the base I am struck by the power and magnitude of this geologic wonder: It has drawn worshippers for hundreds, perhaps thousands, of years. Yet as I climb I am riveted by details, leafy branches escaping from fissures in the stone, water striders skating on transient ponds, shriveled yellow blossoms crowning cacti. Atop, I gaze at buzzards sweeping below me, their circular route gradually shrinking, but I cannot quite pinpoint their prey. I see for many miles in all directions and manage to block out the quarry bustle beyond Moss Lake and the asphalt parking lot somewhere behind me. The sky is cloudless, the sun unrelenting. I nestle under a scraggly mesquite, which casts a pathetic patch of shade, and open a book I deem worthy of this day. I set it aside after struggling with only a few lines. I wonder about prayer and fall asleep.

I doze for only a few minutes: The rock is a harsh pillow.

Why do I commit to making this solo pilgrimage year after year? This has become my ritual, prescribed by no one but myself, serving to punctuate my year. Even as I sit in my driveway in central Austin as the rest of my family heads off to synagogue, I am aware that soon I will experience the magnificence of Enchanted Rock, enter the rhythm of place. I have visited far more spectacular sites in my life: the Colorado Rockies, Norwegian fjords, beaches on Crete. But I am not drawn to Enchanted Rock to bear witness to beauty, to play the tourist focusing through a camera lens. I come here to feel different. I do not come to Enchanted Rock to have my breath taken away; it is not breathtaking scenery that I crave. I come to feel my breath. I need to exert myself, sense my labored breathing as I reach the summit, and feel the heat, my sweat, maybe even the occasional breath of wind against my skin. This is a place to think and not-think. This is a place to sit still. Others find it in synagogue. I find it here.

Tombstone Mountain, Yukon
Territory.

Sam George

The Light at the Top of the World

JOURNAL ENTRY: OCTOBER 13, THURSO
Latitude 58.5°N, longitude 3.5°W. Average air temperature: 43°F. Median water temperature: 45°F. Predominant wind: fresh northwesterly gales off the North Atlantic. Sunrise: 8:30 A.M. Sunset: 4:48 P.M

Surfing in Northern Scotland. I'm alone at the top of the world—a long way from Waikiki. And the color of the top of the world is dark. Forget what the globe tells you—it's not white. White is ice and there's no surf there. On this ocean planet, a surfer's hell is a frozen pole. But here I sit alone in dark water and relive my sins.

The northeastern edge of Thurso Bay has been carved from black slate, layered in slabs, descending into the gray flannel sea. From just below the high tide's highest reach, the stone staircase is carpeted with a layer of purple and green algae, and broad leaves that lie flat against each step as the waters recede. The rolling hills of heather are a dark green, not viridian green, but such a deep shade of green that if you stripped away the outer layer there would be another even more vibrant green beneath. Green you can drown in, even on dry land.

But it's never dry for long in Thurso. Between storms the clouds are still dark and swollen, like the eyes of a woman who's been weeping.

Looming over the east shore is Thurso Castle, built in 1649, now a crumbling ruin. Even with light shining full on its keep and turrets, it's as dark as history—with a lonely emptiness that's seen even from the outside. Thurso Castle is a shadow that ignores the sun, seeping away in inches by the centuries.

October days are dark here, and getting darker, by twelve minutes each day at this latitude. Even the light is dark—rich and oversaturated, like a photo printed with too much red and black. There's no glare, even when the sun is out.

I'm dark, wrapped head to toe in neoprene rubber. Everything in Thurso is dark, except my expression. It's very bright. There are waves here.

Sam George at Thurso, County
Caithness, Scotland.

Activists in one of the last of the great trees. Headwaters Forest Reserve.

Laurence Haston

Away from the Mountain

WELL, HERE I AM AGAIN, underneath Shivling, wonderstruck. The more banal doubts of the mountaineer are easily eclipsed by its sparkling faceted faces. Am I fit enough? What to wear? What gear to take? Am I acclimatized? My companion just stares at the mountain. I can even see its reflection in his ever-so-slightly-crazed eyes. "What shall we take?" I finally ask, knowing what he is going to say anyway. "Let's go light." And so we do.

Five years before it hadn't been so easy. Doubts, insecurity, hesitation, and sickness on the hill. This time, with the tracks of the snow leopard outside the tent this morning, I felt like I couldn't go wrong. Simply stretch my arms and embrace the summit. Well, why not? It's just over there.

Leaving base camp there was no fear as we waved to the holy man. He made a sign and smiled, a smile like the sun warming our clothes and bodies.

Looking back now, months later, with hindsight, thinking of the training I did, running at lunch into the mountain, running back to work, I guess I deserved it. As my friend said, if it seems out of reach, just stand on tiptoe. The summit came and went, not the focal point but the turnaround in the middle of a perfect day, fast and free. The holy man greets us on our return with the mountain in his eyes. Words can describe pain and sweat, but they can't come close to telling you how beautiful Shivling is. With the music of your heart beating away, you return to the world of people, climbers, and base camp. You have descended, literally and metaphorically.

Mount Shivling, India.

Warren Hollinger and Lu Setnicka

Shell Shocked

IT HAPPENED IN AN INSTANT, the explosion in my head. What was happening? I screamed. My partner was screaming too. We were in the midst of an electrical storm one hundred feet below the summit of the west face of the North Howser Tower in the Bugaboos. In an instant I realized we had both been struck by lightning. Amidst the peals of thunder and crackling electricity I couldn't feel anything—it was all noise. I was paralyzed, truly paralyzed, not just immobilized with fear, below the neck. There was nothing we could do but wait it out, an interminable ten hours during which we witnessed two more electrical storms from our cramped ledge while huddling under a port-a-ledge fly. Slowly, sensation came back to my limbs. Time for damage assessment for us both: A bolt had passed through my partner's right butt cheek and out his left thigh, and I had been host to a shock that traveled from the right side of my back to my left knee. My underwear had melted and my pants were riddled with about fourteen tiny holes on the outside. And the holes in my body? I had about seventeen of those, instantly cauterized, clustered about my knee. We pulled out a roll of duct tape to seal the wounds and waited for a break in the storm. The name of our route, a first ascent . . . *Young Men on Fire.*

Lightning striking Half Dome, Yosemite.

Sarah Malarkey

The Secrets of the Night

I AM, strangely enough, on my honeymoon. The past six weeks have transformed me from a soft, shimmering bride to a brown, dirtbag climber. I am happy and strong and feeling pretty tough, so Jonathan and I decide to tackle a direct route on the south face of La Meije. The last Alp to be summitted, La Meije is the most foreboding—and the most tempting—peak in the southern Alps. At 3:00 A.M. we leave our refuge and set out for it laden with ropes, axes, crampons, plastic boots, and pounds of gear and water. The climbing is demanding, and the heavy packs and thin, sharp air slow us down. After twelve hours, we start our descent down the large snowfield that perches on top of La Meije. Its crusted slope tilts steeply toward a two-thousand-foot vertical drop, so we rope up and tread carefully, placing gear in the few wet outcroppings it offers.

On its other side, we breathe deeply, more easily, and start a long set of rappels that will take us to the warmth of a refuge. But the snowfield has soaked our ropes. Wet, they are twice as heavy and impossible to pull through the anchors. Each rappel brings more rope snags, sometimes forcing us to ascend to redo anchors.

I am about to join Jonathan at the bottom of an overhanging rappel when my matted ponytail gets tugged into my figure eight. In an instant, it pulls all the way through, jerking my scalp with it. Suspended by my hair like a cave girl, I kick the air helplessly. I am still a few feet from the ground and too far from the rock to unweight the rope. I hear my scream echo. Jonathan leaps up and with his knife saws through my ponytail, releasing my scalp from its clutch. I collapse onto the ledge, stunned. He tenderly hands me a long, severed clump of hair—hair that just weeks ago had been pulled back, carefully curled, and topped by a wreath of budded roses. My wedding hair. I hold it in my hands and look up. The clouds around us are infused with the blood-red light of sunset. They are wispy clouds, so close to us at this altitude that they seem to embrace. It occurs to me that I have never spent the night outside, climbing. A tough pit inside me cracks open and overflows. I burst into tears and clutch my suddenly light head. Jonathan says urgently, "We are going to spend the night out here. It will be all right."

And he is right. It is just the loss of the sun that makes me so desperate. Once the sky has been drained of all its color, I relax. Nothing has changed so terribly. We can still make our way down under the brackish light of the fat rising moon. Using the headlamp only to check my knots at each rappel, I weight the rope in the dark and kick out blindly against the near vertical gully of rock and ice. Numb, exhausted, shorn, I am pure—an animal using old instincts. It gets late, and the stars move across the arc of sky so fast that it's almost dizzying. Empty, I look up and absorb the beauty of that arcing sky directly, without a snag. I am no longer afraid.

Above: A honeymooner in southern France.

Opposite: Climbing in the Alps.

Ron Matous

Waiting

Squares of ripstop walls.

IT SEEMS TO AFFECT THE EYES more than anything, this constant staring at little squares of ripstop until even the fog that surrounds us is broken into an unrelenting seine of ghostly geometry. If only it would get dark, that would help; but this is June, this is Alaska, and sleep itself is a fading dream.

There are crevasses out there to keep us from entertaining ourselves on our skis: We carefully allot the chapters of our few books to stretch them into the unforeseen future. It is only by chance that we have three small tents instead of one big one, and we have placed them in a long line, door to door, to facilitate the distribution of food as we take turns cooking meals and brewing endless cups of tea, slowly. Only Bruce, whose tent is the one with two doors and thus fell naturally into the middle position, is not entirely happy with the arrangement.

The upper Tokositna glacier is a small, high basin that sits between Mount Hunter and Mount Huntington, not far from the standard landing strip on the Kahiltna, but separated from it by a steep ridge that prevents easy access and holds in the fog. On most days we can hear the periodic drone and whine of planes coming and going with the Denali hordes. Our pilot is probably among them. Once in a while we hear an engine overhead and know that he is looking down on our sea of fog, unable to land. We are waiting.

The only other egress from this hanging valley would be down a monstrous icefall that is squeezed into a narrow slot where the glacier works its way through the peaks. We would sooner eat our boots, which—this being 1978—at least are leather.

It may yet come to that. It has been one foggy week now since we concluded our climb, and the more desirable items on our menu have been consumed. We still have sufficient tuna and bulgur for another week—in fact, sufficient bulgur for a lifetime as far as we're concerned—but the thrill is gone.

By chance, there is another party of three on the Tokositna with us: Glenn, Guy, and Dick, acquaintances from the Tetons who happened to be attempting the same route on Huntington. Now we are all in the same boat. Neither party has anything worth bartering for, and we have long since exhausted the conversational possibilities. Out of respect for the vastness of this glacial wilderness, we have separated our camps by about a hundred yards, just enough to ensure privacy while allowing unroped visitation. We don't do much of that, though: We are waiting.

The eighth day of our vigil dawns clear; salvation is at hand. Our bush pilot flies over in the morning on his way to the Kahiltna and radios to us that he will be able to come in and get us just as soon as he drops off a couple of loads of other climbers. Meanwhile, he requests, we need to get on our skis and stomp out a runway in the soft snow so that he can be sure of taking off again.

We stomp like no one has ever stomped before: half a mile of compacted snow, twenty skis wide, as if we were expecting a fleet of Twin Otters instead of a lone small Cessna. Our gear is packed, our voices animated. In the afternoon, Doug Geeting lands successfully.

Glenn and Dick have been chosen to depart first, though we should all be out today. Stuffed in the fuselage atop duffels and fuel cans, skis and ropes, they wave at those of us left behind as the engine winds high and the little plane taxis down our runway, accelerating out of sight, down-glacier, Talkeetna bound.

Watching for a photo opportunity when the plane rises against the background of Mount Huntington's west face, we can only look at each other when we hear the engine slow and idle for a minute, still out of sight. Then it accelerates again, and this time we see it lift off. We cheer; the photos are magnificent.

We are still standing around by our remaining pile of packs and skis, talking of the showers and steaks to come, celebrating our newfound freedom from the confines of our tents and the horror of bulgur, when we see Doug's two erstwhile passengers trudging disconsolately back up the runway, carrying what they can of the gear that he has dumped. Our runway was inadequate, the snow too softened by afternoon temperatures: Doug says we will have to wait for the freeze-up of early morning.

We can do that, since we have to. But at night the fog returns, and it begins to snow; it will snow for another week. By some miracle the bulgur holds out, though our minds do not; still, we will wait. We will lie in our tents like condemned men, each second a minute, each minute an hour; and slowly the squares of our ripstop walls will become the fabric and pattern of the universe, and the susurration of snow on nylon will become the roar of the Big Bang, still fading, echoing into the distance.

Bob McDougall

Drowning

THE STIKINE IS INDIFFERENT, grayish brown, and cold, as always. The paddle down to Entry Falls is four miles. We beach and hike over for a look. It looks, well, very different from the last time here. Good, actually, runnable—with a punch at the top ledge and then over through a center tongue. I can't quite see into the top drop but decide to go for it. A few warm-up rolls and then I'm in final approach, a tight cliffed-in tunnel with squirrelly side eddies and accelerating water.

The eddy right at the lip is moving pretty good. I back down it a little, and peel out into the current. I turn on the jets, angling with good speed. Dropping over the ledge, I see that I'm in deep, deep trouble. I land upright in the pile and keep pulling hard on the right, but there's no way in hell. I'm slammed back in. Cartwheels interrupted by being wedged with the boat under hydraulics on one side and against a rock on the other. No chance, but I keep fighting it. After another eddy wedge, I fight it off with a wild cartwheel, roll, and new position. I try to work the bow, hoping for a front-ender, twist . . . something. At one point, I think: I hope someone can get out and lower a rope from above. I am exhausted.

Final hurrah, I get turned downstream, pull as hard as I can, but still get perfectly back-ended. With no air left at all, I punch out of the boat. As I come out, my shoes are sucked off. I spank the bottom and then am back in the meat of the hole. I recycle a number of times, it's unclear how many—dark, light, flash of light. I try to breathe, then wham! The boat, too, is in there and we are hammered together. I start going black, little blackouts, and decide I guess I'm going to drown here. I get shoved deep, bounce the bottom really hard, and feel a new thing. I've washed out under something very black. Next, I'm pasted against a rock deep underwater and there is a huge force at my feet pulling me. I don't know which way is down or up or sidewise. I can just make out some light way above my head and then I know that the water is pulling me under a rock to my grave.

I scratch and claw with no air left. Fight now or never fight again. Finally, I start to rise and keep pulling my way to the surface. Then I am spread-eagled on a boulder, sucking oxygen. The surface current is pulling me into the main current. I know I'm not going to survive swimming the rest of the drop but can't stop myself. Inch by inch, the water drags me down the face. The current is whipping by the outer edge. Right at the corner, I slap a little handhold and swing around into a tiny eddy. To the left is a small rock. I gather myself and belly-crawl onto it.

I spend a long time throwing up and drinking in air. I try to stand and prone out again. Then I work my way up to sitting and finally standing. I look at the hole, half expecting to see something—a boat? My lost soul? My equipment is gone. The right slot where the water sucked me under has a log jammed into it, pointing upstream. Terminal. Two or three minutes: my river innocence gone forever.

Soul searching. Bob McDougall on El Rio de las Animas Perdidas.

Thomas McGuane

Twenty-One Beats Twenty

SEA TROUT ARE ENIGMATIC fish to say the least. They are brown trout and therefore subject to that species' notorious moodiness. Sea trout have elicited compulsive fly-changing, night-fishing, pool-stoning, and belly-crawling extremes from their devotees. The sea-run version brings an oceanic rapacity to the smaller world of the river, but they are no easier to understand. We flew into Ciudad Rio Grande in Tierra del Fuego for the promise of favorable full-moon tides. We hoped they would send us fresh waves of such fish.

Our host, Estevan, was by now our old friend. Stevie loved to fish, knew his river well, and kept us amused by his detached sense of humor wherein anglers and all their passions were seen with the objectivity of a good researcher closeted with a houseful of laboratory mice. If one party returned with six fish while another returned with four, Stevie would note, "Six beats four." This later took on a life of its own and Stevie was heard to say, "Eighty-one beats eighty," without any explanation as to what this referred to—though it had to be something other than fish.

His car is a low mountain of caked Tierra del Fuego mud, rod racks on top, rap tapes on the front seat, and a United Colors of Benetton sticker in the rear window. We rumble across the grasslands to the deep, throbbing beat of the Fugees ordering Chinese food in a New York restaurant, sheep fleeing before us in flocks, condor shadows racing from the Andes. Stevie looks around, takes it all in. "Thirty-seven beats twenty-nine."

Yvon believes in going deep. I only go deep when I am utterly discouraged. When Yvon notices me reacting to the sight of his four-hundred-grain shooting head landing on the surface of the Rio Grande like a lead cobra, he states, "To save the river, first I must destroy it." This Pol Pot–style remark fires my determination.

He gets into a pod of bright sea trout and catches one after another with devastating efficiency. Some yards above him, I hold a cold stick, consoling myself despite the cries of my success-gorged partner, "I feel like a shrimper!" The fish must have been running, their silvery rolls and huge boils increasing. At last, I begin hooking up. They are beyond big. They are heavy and violent, taking the fly with malevolence. We are so far into the zone that not even approaching night can drive us out.

A kind of hypnosis results from the long hours of staring into this grasslands river, trying to comprehend its ocean-run fish. I put on a small bomber and begin working the far grassy bank, enjoying the provocative wake the fly pulls behind it. Suddenly, a fish runs my fly down, making an eight-foot rip in the silky flow of

Yvon Chouinard fly-fishing in Rio Nireguao, Patagonia, Chile.

the river. I can feel this one well down into the cork of my doublehander. The fight takes us up and down the pool, and the weight I perceive at the end of my line keeps me on edge. Several times I think I have the fish landed, only to have it power out of the shallows.

In the end, Stevie netted the fish. "Look at those shoulders," he said. We weighed her in the net and Yvon came up for a look; a twenty-five-pound female. To judge by her brilliant silver color and sharp black spots, she was just out of the ocean. Releasing her, I never imagined such a trout belly would ever hang between my two hands. As she swam off the shelf, she pulled a three-foot bow wake. In the sea yesterday, she was going up to the mountains. We watched her go.

Yvon noted that with twenty-one sea-run brown trout, nineteen over fifteen pounds, we had just had the best fishing day we would ever have. We were tired and vaguely stunned. There was almost the sense that wherever we had been going as trout fishermen we had just gotten there. Stevie thought about it all, let his eye follow a flight of ashy-headed geese passing overhead, and said, "Twenty-one beats twenty."

Rio Serrano, Torres del Paine, Chile.

Ellen Meloy

Feral Hunger

We come to Rainbow Bridge down an arduous desert trail from the Navajo Mountain side. The other approach to this popular landmark is much less work. You ride a boat across Lake Powell, the reservoir atop the dammed Colorado River, walk a paved strip from the dock, and behold the soaring ribbon of sandstone. Travelers from both routes meet here, and you can tell which are which. We are not the ones with the cellular phones. The tour-boat people are tidy and refreshed. Despite the long hike my companion retains his quiet grace, as Navajos do, under dust and sweat. Frankly, I look like a yucca plant.

The hike was a cheap piece of procrastination. After long months of river-rangering on a tributary to the east, I extended the season's final float trip with this overland hike, an addendum to the rite of severance from river life. Some reenter civilization slowly, savoring their journeys. I go from sanctuary to techno-shriek in head-on collision, senses flaring. Lunging from one extreme to another eases the pain.

Rainbow Bridge is civilized indeed. Never have I seen so much pantyhose on the north flank of Navajo Mountain. My friend and I sit on a rock nursing blisters, pouring red sand out of our boots, plucking rattlesnakes off our ankles. I am so hungry I could belly up to a grand buffet, then eat the napkins and suck the gravy stains out of the tablecloth. I eat my lunch and half my companion's, then scan the premises for hunting-gathering potential. I suffer this feral hunger whenever I come off a river trip. I cannot exist in Colorado River country unless I take it into myself, then discover it on my very breath. All longing converges on a single piece of geography, my red-rock desert home, whose canyon-bound rivers blaze in sunlight. As I'm poised to hack up and eat ravens with my Swiss Army knife, my friend makes a simple observation. My appetite, he speculates, symbolizes a desire to consume the landscape before I'm torn away from it. There's nothing more impressive than a Freudian Navajo.

We meet our shuttle boat out of Rainbow Bridge and motor to the head of the lake, where a ribbon of Colorado River spills into it. On the highway headed out, I crane my neck to keep the river in view until the last curve obliterates it. I turn and face the road. I'm no longer hungry. Already I'm dying of starvation.

Rainbow Bridge National Monument, Utah.

Heart of Darkness.

Dave Olsen

Opposed at the Equator

I ENTER THE CANOPY ALONE. My boots attack the hard red soil. Then: a crashing thud. What the . . . ? Thud! Thud! The ground jumps and so do my nerves. I freeze, unable to place the sound in the late-afternoon gloom. Foolish to make this trek so unprepared, without at least an Ibo companion. So at home in trackless northern forests and here so—thud—uneasy on a well-worn trail.

"Get low," I tell myself as my colonial fantasies of untamable jungle race uncontrolled. "Blend into the background. Try not to look like fresh meat." I sit, to slow down to the rhythm of the life around me—and until I figure out who or what is making the ground shake.

At dusk I string my hammock and netting. It's at least a three-hour walk to the next village and I know I can't find my way in the dark. The bug sounds build— a cicadalike background hum. The rhumba of giant crickets. Alto-pitched locusts. Shrill whines close to my ears. The intermittent thuds have long since been drowned out. As the blackness closes in, the monkeys advance their screeching taunts. Jagged bird shrieks sear the cacophony. The charged clangor pulses, magnetic, impenetrable. It is thrilling to the bone.

And it wires me awake. The snakes I saw in the trees today coil into the edges of my consciousness. Constant crashes worry the underbrush. Unknown mammals scream. The steamy swamp shrinks generations into hours, as riotous growth and death whirl around me. I am terrified, the price of being more adventurous than wise, and very out of place.

Four degrees north of the equator, the immense Niger Delta unravels its river, muddy and turbulent, into the sea. Far upstream, the Strong Brown God widely ribbons through the fastnesses of Mali and the length of Nigeria, desert giving way to jungle and in turn to mangrove swamp. Down the innumerable branchings of the delta, it dissolves into the Gulf of Guinea, two hundred kilometers away from my dark hammock.

Not long ago the Republic of Biafra sprang up here, seceding from Nigeria, and was soon bombed and starved into submission. A pathetic tribal conflict, Western capitals cried—crocodile tears for the underdeveloped world, obscuring steely concern for control of the vast cache of oil underlying the struggle.

I've come with big questions. Did Nigeria get covert help to crush Biafra? How, exactly, do industrial powers ensure access to resources everywhere in this age of independent states?

But tonight, the raucous wild rips at the purposes that marched me here. Unable through my own primitive imaginings to see the individuality of the life around me and fearful of what I don't understand, I grasp at the wish for dominion, to contain the creatures crowding in, to end the uncertainties of the stifling night. Caught in my fragile netting, I can't escape in myself the same control-craving colonialism I've come to expose.

Uneasily aware, I wonder at the people who know the ways of this place, its mysteries and beauty and danger. I try to imagine a way of being in the world so different from my own. The night accelerates again, mocking me as the minutes edge by.

Toward morning, the animal sounds die down. Then: thud! It returns. I twist to sit up and get caught in my hammock. To my left, a dark presence emerges from the receding blackness. As I begin to make out the gargantuan tree, an enormous white blossom falls from above my head. It must be more than eighteen inches across, I think, as it plunges past me to the ground. Thud.

Then another huge corolla rockets down. Thud. It must weigh five pounds; the ground shakes with the impact. I almost laugh. I've been unnerved by the wilt of a tree.

As I pack my hammock, the flowers falling heavily everywhere around me, I struggle to make sense of the exploding fecundity that has raced my own growth through the night. I'll leave this jungle still opposed to the "development" that threatens its transfixing life. But it will be with very different eyes.

Five-thousand-foot descent into Batopilas Canyon, Sierra Madre, Mexico.

Left: Star trails over Cordon Cactus
Camp, Baja.

Right: Simon Mentz and Steve Monks on
the Totem Pole. Cape Hauy, Tasmania,
Australia.

Forty Yards of Separation

IT WAS A STUPID, exaggerated white-water rebound; no one even there to see it. Bogged the rail coming off the soup, grabbed for the tailblock and felt it slip through chilled fingers. Then I was swimming toward the shore of Namibia's Skeleton Coast. Alone in the fifty-five-degree water, twenty minutes past sundown, and the nearest town a hundred miles south. Half a mile away was a colony of eighty thousand fur seals. Most predator-prey ratios are something like a thousand deer per one grizzly, so I knew somewhere out there along the shelf there had to be at least one whitey pulling my file for review.

The Skeleton Coast is the North Shore of shipwrecks. From the lineup at the cape no less than three were visible; desolate bone-piles of ribbing and keels and leprous rusty boilers. Technically I was shipwrecked myself. I'd been separated from my vessel and was swimming to safety on one of the most bleak coastlines in the world, like thousands before me who had traded the cold butchery of the sea and sharks for the agonies of thirst and madness on the parched desert shore.

Hard-boiled New Yorkers say that when walking at night through a bad neighborhood you must exude confidence and take purposeful, aggressive strides so as to lessen your profile as a potential victim. I tried to swim with leisurely indifference, radiating invulnerability: "I'm an alpha-seal, Mr. Whitey. Leave me be."

Fifty yards now. I could see my board pinging around in a small rock pool. A ways down the beach some fishermen had lit lanterns on poles over their trucks as they stowed gear and the day's catch. Cozy, safe. Civilization. Suddenly a warm towel, that evening's hot meal, and cold beer shared with friends seemed impossibly sweet and desirable.

Forty more yards. Forty yards was the difference between being in the Triassic food chain 100 million years distant and warming cold feet in an automobile speeding toward a hot pizza. I sucked another lungful of air, put my head down, and swam for home.

Dave off the top in Namibia.

Doug Peacock

Damage Control

Coyote caught in a number-three trap.

In November of 1990, Marc Gaede (*Bordertowns, Images from the Great West*) stopped by my home in Tucson. Gaede, a fine photographer who was, at the time, working on a picture book on "radical environmentalists," wanted to take a picture of me releasing a coyote from a trap. This was troubling.

I hadn't intended on making any kind of career out of freeing coyotes from federal Animal Damage Control steel-jawed traps with my bare hands, three inches from the wild canine's jaws. The first one had been an accident.

In 1990, on my way to collect mesquite cooking wood in a sadly overgrazed valley east of the Picacho Mountains, I stumbled across a coyote caught in a number-three trap connected to a chain leading to a rebar grappling hook attached to a mesquite tree. I slowly approached and the coyote, naturally figuring I was his tormentor coming to kill him, charged violently and desperately, then dislocated his paw tugging back away from me. At ten feet I stopped and spoke in a low, calm voice to show I meant him no harm. After a few minutes—with me not moving—the young coyote ceased his futile lunges.

I moved in slowly, a half step at a time, talking to the coyote constantly, much like I talk to grizzly bears. It took me at least ten minutes to reach the trap. I knelt and reached out toward it with my bowie knife, trying to pry apart the steel jaws. The spring was too strong; I couldn't open it. The animal leaned away from me. I dropped the knife and moved forward. I took the trap in my hands. The coyote took a step toward me and sat down, one paw raised (caught in the trap that I now held) like my old collie dog used to do. I worked my fingers into the steel jaws and touched his mangled paw. I pulled against the spring and opened the trap. The wounded coyote—sitting on his haunches, paw in the air, his nose only four inches from my own—didn't move a muscle. I leaned slowly into his face and whispered, "go." My little brother—God's dog—vanished into the creosote.

That day I let go two more coyotes from ADC traps. Later, I released four more. Sometimes it takes twenty or thirty minutes to quiet them down. Other times taming doesn't work and I just cut their chains with bolt cutters. But it can be done. I did it.

The hard part was explaining to Marc Gaede why he couldn't take a picture of me freeing wild coyotes from traps. I'm not exactly shamanistic or any kind of hippie, but there is a non-Euclidean side to this stuff. The purity of your intentions might be important.

Maybe it's something about karma. I told Marc it was a bad idea, that if we went out there for the purpose of taking a photograph of me releasing coyotes from ADC traps, the coyote would likely bite my goddamn face.

Mark Renneker, M.D.

Staying Dry in the Aleutians

AS A PHYSICIAN WORKING with people facing life-threatening illnesses, I've learned that each of us carries from childhood some place in the world that we've always wanted to go, that those places are invariably cold and weird and rarely thought of as tourist destinations, and that our lives may depend on someday going there. Maybe it was the sound of the name of the place that initially grabbed you, having heard it during a story read or told to you; regardless, it became embedded. Places such as Tierra del Fuego, Tasmania, Labrador, Spitsbergen, Kamchatka, and, for me, the Aleutians. As a beginning surfer, at age eleven, when I'd heard that name and learned the Aleutians produce the world's largest, most beautiful waves, it became my place. It took me thirty-five years, though, to finally get there, in October 1997, on what was to be the first ever full-fledged Aleutian surfing expedition.

After a harrowing landing at the jumping-off point within the Aleutians, Dutch Harbor (dicey landings there are legendary, I was told, due to ferocious winds), then a horrifying local reconnaissance flight to look for surf (the worst flight I've ever been on, aborted due to katabatic winds), and, finally, finding no boat under a hundred feet willing to venture out of harbor (because of the fierce, non-stop Bering Sea winds), I knew I was in the right place: Wind equals swell. After being stuck in Dutch for a week, on a rare calm day I managed to charter a plane to fly us down-chain to the island of Umnak, near the small town of Nikolski, whose surrounding volcanic reefs had been my focus of study (on marine charts) for months.

I'd brought with me a semi-shivering group of fellow surfers, who to varying degrees shared my Aleutian obsession. We delighted in the fact that the first Umnak beach we came to had an obviously world-class wave—not huge, but nearly perfect—so there we camped, already feeling utterly accomplished. We'd scored, big time! But still, my reason for coming seemed incomplete.

There is a pervasive sense of brooding in the Aleutians. The generally gray sky, the deadly, still active volcanoes, the sheer black cobalt cliffs, the treeless, endless moors, the lack of people. It's lonely. It feels like death. Huddled in Nikolski are only sixty or so Aleuts, but their people have been there for the past four thousand years; Nikolski is the oldest continuously occupied town in North America. To live so long in such a harsh place, the Aleuts became the ultimate wilderness outfitters. Long before Gore-Tex and Polartec, the Aleuts made waterproof pants and jackets from the tongue skin of whales and the esophagus and intestines of sea lions. It's not surprising then that, given their knowledge of anatomy, they had sophisticated mummification practices. Eviscerated and carefully maintained, the dead were

regularly conversed with and often continued "living" in the house, eventually becoming what was called a "dry one." After a time, the dry ones were placed long-term in warm, volcanic gas-heated caves, and were then visited for help and advice as the need arose.

One of the Aleuts from Nikolski, Peat, explained to me that in 1874 the mummies had been taken from their caves on nearby Kagamil Island by an American captain, and that they now "lived" in Washington, D.C., in the Smithsonian. One of these mummies was named Little Wren. Peat had never been to the Lower 48, he said, and he was thinking of finally going, but only to Washington, D.C., because he needed to talk to Little Wren about something.

The Aleutians, the place I'd gone to, had come home to me: Of the people I've worked with and the people I've loved who are now dead, I felt freer than ever to sometimes talk with them.

Aleutians surf camp. A chatroom for Raven.

Awakenings

I AM THIRTEEN YEARS OLD. I live in a small town in California that allows you to not think about some of the problems you see in other parts of the world. I have learned about pollution, overpopulation, vanishing ozone, and the destroyed habitats of creatures I will never get to see. Prior to last summer, however, I had never felt how fragile it all is. I had never felt the urgency to be protective.

Last summer I spent one month in the Sierra learning about leave no trace backpacking. Gradually I came to realize the impact humans have had on the earth. I began to see anything added or taken away by humans as a mistake.

At the end of the month, my family took me on a car-camping trip through southern Utah. As we drove, my big sister read *The Monkey Wrench Gang* aloud. I gazed out the window at miles of paved road, bridges, electric and telephone wires, lakes drained to provide water for L.A., cities in the desert, and grazing cows where buffalo had been. My sister read on and on. I became more and more outraged.

We went to Bryce, Zion, Capitol Reef, the Grand Canyon; the beauty and grandeur took my breath away. And then Lake Powell came slowly into view. It was completely surreal, like Disneyland on the moon; an enormous sparkling lake in the middle of the desert with speedboats and water-skiers. Then the consequence, the Colorado River. It lay dead, green, and stagnant beneath us. We were approaching the Glen Canyon Dam. I got out of the car and walked across it. I imagined what it must have been like on this earth before humans started constructing things. I imagined rivers running free, blue skies, and tall forests. A world without concrete and steel. A peregrine falcon swooped overhead.

My sister and my little brother, inspired by *The Monkey Wrench Gang*, said, "Let's blow up the dam and every bulldozer we see." I considered what my dad says: "It's like eating an elephant; take one bite at a time," and decided I would find out what I could about what a person can do to help restore the Glen Canyon.

I discovered that in 1996, because of a grassroots effort, a decision was made to establish an Adaptive Management Program for the Glen Canyon Dam that considers the river's needs as well as people's needs. The goal is to reestablish a free-flowing Colorado River, restore Glen Canyon, drain Lake Powell, and finally decommission Glen Canyon Dam.

We can't give up hope about our future. We can't say "forget it, it's too late" and head out to Lake Powell and jet ski around. We all have to get involved and take care of the earth we live on. As Thoreau said, "Now. Or never." The first step is to become aware of what humankind has done and is doing to our planet. The next step is to get involved and help in whatever way you can. Be passionate and tireless. For inspiration, all you need is a day in the wilderness.

Above: Cameron descending Mount Whitney.

Opposite: Letting go, Havasu Falls, Grand Canyon.

Rick Ridgeway

A Jungle Mirror

A FEW YEARS AGO, we climbed a remote rock tower in the upper Orinoco. On an expedition such as this, the quest for the summit is more an excuse for the journey. We hired porters from two tribal groups: the more Westernized Yekuana, and the wild Yanomami. We'd wanted to take all Yanomami, but we'd been warned by "old jungle hands" in Caracas that the Yanomami did not understand the Western concept of work for hire. As we were going into an uninhabited region, the hunting was sure to be excellent: If the Yanomami sighted game, they might drop their loads and disappear for days. We hired fourteen Yekuana and five Yanomami.

We spent the first week in dugouts traveling upriver. I shared a boat with two Yanomami, and one day, one of them, looking for a place to nap, curled up in my lap. At first I withdrew. But then, realizing my reaction was acculturated, I relaxed, draped my arm over his shoulder, and noticed he smelled like sweet oil and that his skin was cool against my legs. In a few minutes, he was asleep.

Each day the tributaries narrowed. We lay in the boats watching the jungle squeeze out the open sky until finally the canopy closed over. We shored the boats and started overland through untracked jungle, a walk that would take about a week.

On the second day, I was following a Yanomami, naked except for a single crimson loincloth, when he suddenly dropped his pack and with bow and arrow dashed into the jungle. "There goes the first one," I thought as I dropped my own pack and quickly followed.

Through an opening in the understory of spindly trees, I caught sight of him standing in a shaft of light with his bow poised. Then I heard them: a troop of monkeys perhaps one hundred yards distant. The Yanomami made a monkey call, then hunched over and began a monkey pantomime. I stared, transfixed.

The monkeys, curious, moved in to get a closer look, and at the critical moment, the Yanomami pulled his bow and released an arrow. Whoosh! The monkeys went wild; the shot missed. The Yanomami turned and looked right at me— the first indication that he knew I was there—and smiled and laughed.

A few days later, we arrived at the base of the spire. When we started the first pitches up the steep granite, the Yanomami, watching us, laughed. To them, our antics were really funny. The climb progressed, and at night, lying on bivouac ledges overlooking the jungle, I would recall the Yanomami and the monkey dance, and once when I reconstructed the vision fully it again gave me a chill. There was something about it I couldn't shake.

It wasn't until I returned to my own world that I figured it out. In that shaft of light in the jungle, I'd watched the Yanomami transform into a wild animal. For the first time in my life, I had seen *Homo sapiens*. I had seen who I used to be.

Yanomami tribesman, upper Orinoco River.

The long road to Seneca.

Don Roberts

Backcountry Boogie

GORED MIDSTREAM . . .

My battered, blue '59 Chevy pickup shudders like a mortally wounded ox. I pull as far off the steep canyon road as I dare and kill the engine. Having just forded a creek, water drips from the truck's undercarriage and it's now listing severely to starboard, both tires on that side slit through cleanly.

I walk back a few paces and examine the innocent gurgling brook. A steel spike, the type used to secure loads on log trucks, juts from the streambed, its point barely visible below the soft trill of water.

The odds of anyone else soon rumbling down this remote side canyon are about the same as for the Chicago Cubs winning the next pennant. After all, isolation was the prime reason for being here in the first place. That and redband trout. According to the topo map, the closest hint of civilization, the micro-town of Seneca, lies seventeen miles to the northwest, more than half of that cross-country, eventually intersected by a seldom-used Forest Service road. I grab only my wallet and a water bottle and start hoofing.

The northern extreme of the Great Basin is a scabrock playa carved out of nothingness, a place of basalt buttes, blind canyons, parched arroyos, and a lot of very little in between. A place nourished by tenuous streams that advance and retreat with the vagaries of winter snowpack and spring cloudbursts—one of the last refuges of the reclusive redband trout. While traipsing this broad barren, I pass the time by replaying the memory loops of each redband trout that had risen to my fly.

As I near the summit of Stinking Water Pass, the sun impales itself on a jagged escarpment, then bleeds out in the shimmering sky, the sanguine finality of day on the high desert. Pressing on, I reach the Forest Service road just before nightfall, the light failing amid a calm so deep you can hear hair grow. The road bears west, flat, hard, and featureless. The darkness is seamless and mute, except for the occasional breathy wing beat of a passing owl. Slave to a mind-numbing cadence, I reach Seneca in four hours.

The entire settlement appears to be locked up tight, perhaps permanently; it's hard to tell in the anemic glow of the town's one and only streetlight. But down the road a piece, I can see the neon and feel the electric hum of the local alehouse, the Gouge Eye Saloon. One must observe protocol when encountering strange taverns in the hinterlands. Inch your face through the door and survey the premises. Do not enter if (1) there is blood congealing on the floor, (2) there is blood congealing on a patron, or (3) your gaze is met by the squint-eyed grins of a silent mob.

Given the scarcity of alternatives, I mosey on into the Gouge Eye with the thirsty resolve of a dust-drenched local. A blind-drunk codger in a Stetson is shouting repeatedly to an uninterested clientele, "I'm an old cowhand from the Rio Grande." Another regular promptly orders me the specialty of the house: a gen-uu-wine, home-forged spicy-hot pickle, served in a soggy paper towel. More than a mere welcoming gesture, this is some kind of backwoods initiation rite. I raise it in salute and commence chomping, fighting back tears as the incendiary condiment detonates in my esophagus. My satisfied benefactor yells, "fire extinguisher, fire extinguisher!" and the bartender thunks down two frosty mugs of Blitz.

After the requisite interval of silence and beer sipping, I ask about a phone. The bartender reaches under the counter and sets an old rotary-dial phone right next to my beer glass. I push a couple of frogskins across the bar and he pushes them right back. "You ain't gonna talk that long, not at this hour you ain't," he winks.

The phone ringing at the other end of the line is only a couple mountain passes away, yet it sounds galactically distant. Finally, a sleepy voice answers. I explain the situation, give directions and coordinates. "Yeah, Seneca. The Gouge Eye Saloon. No, no, I'm not kidding. Seneca . . . off Highway 395, north of Burns. You know, near the north fork of the Malheur. Yeah, you'll need a map."

Her voice trails off drowsily, then, as if to verify this isn't really a dream, she asks through a yawn, "Where did you say?"

As I wander outside for a breath of air, raindrops as big as gooseberries burble against the pavement. A group of teenage boys is gathered around a '63 Impala. The doors are open, the motor is running, and two quart bottles of Oly are set on the roof. They are laughing and horsing around with a nickel-plated revolver.

One of the young Turks notices me standing there. He has a protruding brow ridge and thin-lidded dull-cast eyes. "Hey, muh-fuh, whaddya starin' at?" he accuses.

I feel raindrops thudding on my shoulders, "Nothing really," I answer. "Had a couple. Ate a pickle. That's all." We regard each other in the rain-spattered darkness. Then I shrug. "What else is there?"

Nanga Parbat—A Winter Attempt

En route on Nanga Parbat.

THERE IS AN UNSPOKEN Alpine climbing manifesto that goes like this:

If you are not hungry, you are carrying too much food.

If you are warm, you have too many clothes.

If you are not frightened, you have too much gear.

If you get up your climb, it was too easy anyway.

If you are into Alpine climbing, you have to spend much of your time being cold, hungry, and frightened. And you have to fail occasionally. The best climbs, according to Mick Fowler, are those you either "just" get up or "just" fail to complete. But sometimes you miss by a mile, and still there will be lessons to learn.

And sometimes you have stupid ideas. This idea of ours just may have been one of those. We had noticed that none of the Pakistani eight-thousand-meter peaks had been climbed in winter. So our idea, which was born in a pub in Alyth, a small village in north Scotland, was to mount a winter expedition to one of them. The single malt whiskey was excellent, the fireplace glowing, and the mountains seemed far away.

There are five eight-thousand-meter peaks in Pakistan. Four of them, K2, Broad Peak, and the Gasherbrums, have to be approached by the long Baltoro Glacier, which in winter proves to be a logistical nightmare. By contrast, Nanga Parbat can be reached in three days from the roadhead at any time of year. We discussed the different faces of the mountain. The Rupal Face had the benefit of facing south but was too technical for a very small group and would probably need lots of fixed rope. The original route climbed in 1954 by Hermann Buhl would be too long, but the Diamir Face was interesting. Alfred Mummery had reached a point maybe halfway up the face in 1895, following a trio of red buttresses. In 1939, Heinrich Harrer reconnoitered a couloir to the left of the Mummery line. His expedition ended in internment by the British and his subsequent escape to Tibet. The Harrer line was eventually climbed in 1962 by Kinshoffer, and this looked like the obvious line for us. The main difficulties were low down, and it seemed they could be dealt with Alpine style, with no fixed ropes or permanent camps. It also seemed a logical and sensible thing to try the first winter ascent with a two-man team.

We were quite wrong, of course, but we could not know that at the time: After all, no one else had tried a two-man winter ascent of the mountain. Someone had to go first.

I won't go into the details of the climb, except to say that it was cold. Not any colder than Alpine winter climbing can be, but then in the Alps you retire after a day or two to a nice, warm hut and drink gallons of hot coffee. By contrast, we were

twelve days out from base camp, in a working temperature of minus thirteen to minus thirty-one degrees. The ice screws sometimes failed to go in, the heads collapsing under the strain and twisting into useless spirals of titanium, disturbingly similar to one of those sardine cans that opens with a key. The crampons did not bite more than a fraction of an inch into the ice, and anything metallic had to be kept well away from unprotected skin.

None of that was new to us. My climbing partner, Rafael Jensen, a Dane now settled in Sweden, had spent time in the Antarctic, while I had knocked around the Alps in winter quite a bit. Nor was the altitude new to us. We first had met 7,800 meters on K2. It did mean that it was difficult to maintain body heat. Metabolism is a less effective warming device in low levels of oxygen. Nor was the prolonged outing new; we had done this before—day after day, night after night, hauled our means of survival slowly uphill like a pair of optimistic snails. It was the combination of all these factors that was new to us.

In the end we were worn down by the constant triple hauling, the constant battle to keep warm, and the need to climb fifty-five-degree ice, pitch by pitch. It was entertaining in a grim sort of way. We woke up each morning in a deep freeze, ice caked around the opening of the sleeping bag, an inch of sugar frost on the inside of the tent. The first hour was spent making the first brew of the day, the next making some kind of food and defrosting our inner boots, which froze while inside the sleeping bags.

We had no sun for four days, and in that time, ice condensed inside our sleeping bags until they became no more than two sheets of nylon and lumps of frozen down. Slowly it became clear that we were not going to make it. I started having nightmares that reflected my nagging, persistent fear of frostbite. During the day, I dreamed of reaching the summit slopes, elation driving me past exhaustion. At those moments I would look around, consider just how hostile our environment was, and wonder which was the real madness, the daydreams or the nightmares.

Well, as they say, some you lose. We learned a few lessons. Lessons about pushing oneself to the limit, about winter Himalayan climbing with a team of just two. Rafael had said at the beginning of the trip, "I don't know if we're going to succeed, but I am going to give my body hell trying." Finally we learned a lesson about the manifesto: We had been cold, hungry, and frightened. By the end we were tired too; another lesson, and that was good.

It is good to fail sometimes. It teaches one humility. If the problems we set for ourselves are not to be trivial, failure is a normal part of mountaineering, and a normal part of life.

In the North Atlantic.

David Scully

Sailing Alone

THE SEA IS SHROUDED in the impenetrable white, cold breath of the Labrador current. Like liquid oxygen, or some gaseous form of snow, it settles on exposed surfaces, freezing and wet. Caused by the confluence of warm air rising northward and Arctic waters driven south by the current, it sits like a feathery cap on the head of the North Atlantic, a fog engine producing its frigid essence regardless of wind and weather.

My small boat sailed under its skirts some days ago, driven by one of a series of depressions that wrack the Great Circle route between England and the States. I am racing alone from Plymouth, England, to Newport, Rhode Island, a competitor in the Single-Handed Transatlantic Race. The warm Devon shore, the pre-race parties, the oft-repeated farewells and good-luck wishes from friends and fellow racers are ten days old, but that happened on another planet. Since the Lizard dropped below my VHF radio horizon, it has been me and the sea.

Now we are about as far from anywhere as one can be in the North Atlantic. Greenland is one thousand miles to the north; the Azores the same distance to the south. The nearest port is St. John's, Newfoundland, twelve hundred miles to the west.

I am below in the tiny cabin of my thirty-footer, chart on my knee, reviewing this information because things are not going well. For the past several hours, the mainsail has been on deck. I have been gripping the boom with my elbows as the boat rolls from beam to beam, sewing miles of reinforcing tape over a long vertical tear that appeared in the mainsail leach during the gale of the last few days. The violent motion of the boat has also taken its toll on the autopilots. I started with three. Now two have gallantly ground their bearings to powder in an effort to maintain course and speed in the rough weather. One remains, for what may well be over two thousand miles left of sailing.

I recall the misery of the BOC race around the world when, alone, I was forced to hand-steer for six days due to faulty pilots. Driving for twelve hours at a stretch. Heaving to for half an hour to eat, pee, and bail out the boat. The boat was bigger, the conditions milder. I cannot see hand-steering on the open deck of *Hot Glue Gun,* dashed every minute with a double bucketful of three-degree Labrador current, for days on end. This is the way to exhaustion, which leads to mistakes, which leads, at sea, to loss of control, then to death.

My fear, as I considered the options, was not yet loss of my ship or my life. My overwhelming concern was losing a mile to the pack of boats I guessed to be about thirty miles astern. Torn sails and faulty pilots are competitive disadvantages, and after the months of work and planning I had invested in my boat and the race, I hated, above all things, to see my chances of a win eroded.

Then I remembered the most important lesson a solo sailor can learn. It had happened in the Southern Ocean. High on the forestay, a tiny screw had begun to undo. Eventually, it would jeopardize the sail, the rig, and my chances of reaching my destination. Try as I might, and I tried many and dangerous ways, I could not reach it. I sat on the deck, despairing, thinking, "It's impossible."

But it had to be repaired. How does one do the impossible?

The answer that came to me was, "One step at a time."

The first problem to solve was how to get to the spot. The forestay had already proved an impossible ascent. Using spinnaker poles, I managed to construct a sort of scaffolding upon which I could climb high enough to get at the screw. A half pint of Loctite later, we were back in the race.

A few days later the same thing happened, even higher in the rig. The repair was easy.

As I remembered that lesson, I began counting the things that were going right for me. I was leading. I had a working pilot. The sail problem was reparable. My boat was sound and I was in good form.

Given these advantages, the problems could be overcome. I could drive for four-hour stretches, sixteen hours a day, during bad weather, thus relieving the pilot. Calm weather would allow me to effect repairs and catch up on my sleep. As for the sail, I had plenty of thread. If it continued to break, I would continue to sew.

Anne Smith

Faith

Anne Smith on Ama Dablam.

FAITH IN THE MOUNTAIN and faith in myself were how I began the summer. I was going to the Himalayas in the fall to climb the southwest ridge of Ama Dablam (22,500 feet)—not very high compared to its neighbors, but a classic, beautiful route, and my first in Nepal. Alpine climbing and long-distance running have always been the closest I've ever come to religion. Up high on a névé slope with the evening wash of light on the distant peaks, air filling my lungs and blood pumping through my body, is when I believe.

I live in Ophir, Colorado, at 10,000 feet: the perfect training ground for the climb. Ophir sits in a valley flanked by 13,000-foot summits, a criss-cross of old mining roads, and an 11,500-foot pass leading out one end to the town of Silverton. Out my front door is wilderness where I can run forever and see no one—I call out once in a while to frighten the bears and bull elk from crashing across my path.

The goal of the mountain gave me direction: how and what kind of running to do. I would need to endure for long lengths of time over uncertain ground up high in thin, thin air. A good run for me would average ten miles, last a couple of hours, and always go up. My favorite loop went into Waterfall Canyon: shady single-track smelling of sunbaked pine needles, wading through snowmelt streams and patches of willows, topping out on the upper rim, crossing snow patches, through fields of wildflowers with marmots chirping all the way. Up top with my skin tingling, my head light, my shoes soaked from the thick dew, I felt light and good and clean and strong. These runs became my personal communion, my daily mass.

It usually took me about twenty minutes to forget myself, to become the motion, to enter the state where I almost lost consciousness of what I was doing. My mind and body became the rhythm, the breathing, the snow, or the rock. I've read about "flow," about entering "the zone," and about endorphin highs. I guess that's what it is, but for me, it's a time when I don't have to be myself for a while, and I can become a part of something else. I have never been good at the short quick bursts of strength required for sport climbing or sprinting. It can't be indoors or on pavement. It can't be in the city, and there can't be people around. It has to be long and in the mountains. Sure, it hurts—burning lungs and muscles, making myself get to the next tree or boulder—but it's a pain that means something. I become a zealot for that mental and physical place.

When we were finally on Ama Dablam, seventeen-hour days were not uncommon. I would climb and be lost in it, often alone, winding for hours around and over granite gendarmes, through hourglasses of ice or up endless snow steps along mushroom ridges. Light shone through a red and navy stained-glass sky, and the halo of mountains glowed. If ever, this was my prayer.

Body surfer watching the door close at
Sandy Beach, Oʻahu.

Jim Snyder

Butterflies

I FIRST WITNESSED IT back in the seventies, in the foam below Rivers' End rapid. Within arm's reach, a butterfly flew out of the foam.

A few years later several of us marveled at it again at Wonder Falls. This time we saw several butterflies. They would dart about the fringe of the misty vapors made brilliant by sunlight. Suddenly they would willfully become one with the falls by flying in from the side. Eternal moments later they would fly out. Their transition to airborne was seamless. Before long they would go at it again, always emerging unscathed.

I've only seen this a few times. It always happens in bright sunlight and leaves me speechless, though full of questions. What protects them in the torrents? How do they navigate their precise entry in this vast, powerful arena with their limited sight? Can a butterfly be brave? I don't think this dance is vital to their survival—until they make it so. And yet they seem compelled to put their frail existence on the line for a few moments of glory as they blend with the falls. Was I seeing a work of Joy or the deceptions of Destruction? And why would Nature see fit to have me witness this? What does this mean to them? Are they participating in Profound Serendipity? And what would aliens think if they saw me playing in my squirt boat? One thing may explain it all. Universal Fun.

Spirit Falls, Little White Salmon River.

Getting a leg up on the off-width "Flight
Line," South Rim, Grand Canyon.

Angel on High

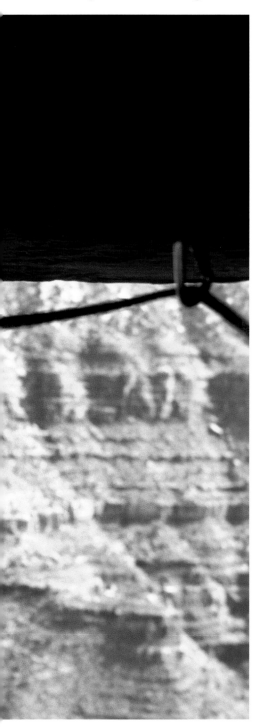

THE SOUTH FACE of Yosemite's Washington Column is a classic introduction to big-wall climbing: five strenuous aid pitches, five moderate free pitches, a cavernous roof, and a palatial bivy ledge with a stunning view of Half Dome. We studied all the guidebooks, bought or borrowed the gear, and with enough determination to match our anxiety, we started our ascent.

Belaying Johnny on the second pitch, I heard another climber behind us and looked over to see a youthful face framed by a set of brown pigtails. Clad in thrift-shop clothing, she hoisted a massive haulbag to the belay. I waited to see her partner, but none arrived. She set her bag next to me and began to coil her rope. "What route are you doing?" she asked.

"The South Face," I replied. "And you?"

"I'm soloing Skull Queen," she said, and resumed her coiling.

I spent the next five minutes trying to remember anything I might have read about Skull Queen, at the same time marveling that one so small and angelic could be soloing a big wall. Eventually, I remembered that Skull Queen was the steep route that branches off from the South Face after the Kor Roof: The guidebook mentioned that the route required knifeblades, Lost Arrows, hooks, and rivet hangers. While I was trying to remember the difference between a knifeblade and a Lost Arrow—and just what is a rivet hanger anyway?—Aimee introduced herself and asked if we would mind trailing a rope for her.

By the time we reached Dinner Ledge two pitches later, Aimee had become our mentor. She was the how-to book we left at home, offering us advice when we needed it and filling the time with tales of her big-wall exploits. She'd done the South Face, the Prow, Leaning Tower, and Zodiac on El Capitan. She'd just graduated from college and wanted to do a couple more routes on El Cap before the end of summer. She didn't seem to mind being smaller than her haulbag.

Our plan was to eat lunch, then fix two pitches above Dinner Ledge before rappelling back to the ledge for the night. We each ate a slice of cold pizza and I roped up to lead the straightforward but strenuous Kor Roof pitch. I flailed and worked too hard for a while, but by the last of four bolts, I was climbing more efficiently. I stepped over the roof to find a long crack slanting right and up to a belay that seemed a mile away.

After twenty-eight placements and three hours, I reached that belay and looked down at Johnny and Aimee, lounging on Dinner Ledge. Johnny cleaned the pitch quickly, with Aimee offering hints on how to clean a roof and a traverse. She saved Johnny hours of frustration by suggesting that he clip an aider to the piece above the one he was trying to clean and weight it, thus enabling him to unclip

On the summit.

the nearest piece without experiencing a terrifying swing.

After we fixed Aimee's rope to the belay, Johnny started up the next pitch, turning another roof and then traversing left. I looked down and noticed Aimee ascending her rope, spinning around in the void below the roof. She glided up her line with a graceful efficiency that I could only hope to achieve. Within minutes, she met me at the belay and prepared to solo her next pitch. When I looked up, Johnny was at the next belay. After I cleaned the pitch, we rappelled the fixed line back to the ledge, descending into a landscape dominated by the sunset glow on Half Dome.

Back again on Dinner Ledge, we surveyed the valley below and relished our elevated perch. We finished the pizza, guzzled water, and marveled at the play of the waning sunlight on the granite all around us. Aimee broke out in a soft song that seemed to welcome the darkness. I drifted off, anxious for tomorrow but relishing this moment of relaxation. Our fixed line, shooting to the sky, fed my dreams.

I awoke to the sound of Aimee packing her haulbag and preparing to jug her fixed rope. Johnny and I watched our mentor work her way gracefully up the rope. Would we see her again? Should I ask for an address? She stopped for a moment below the roof as if to enjoy spinning around on a single strand in midair, then looked down at us with a grin and said, "Look me up next time you're in the valley. I park my Subaru in the Sunnyside parking lot. Montana plates." She then turned and resumed her upward glide.

Ulua

Rell paddling out.

"'A'OHE IA E LOA'A AKU, HE ULUA KAPAPA NO KO MOANA."
Literally: "He cannot be caught, for he is an ulua *fish of the deep ocean."*
Said in admiration of a warrior who will not give up without a struggle.

Reaction time is faster when you see bigger fish. At the instant I saw the forty-five-pound *ulua* munching on a tiny snowflake eel, my Hawai'ian sling hand-spear was already cranked and flying. The three prongs lodged in the back of his blunt head and he spun once, eyeing me with reproach, but instead of screeching for the channel, he turned back to the eel. I was faster and luckier with my backup spear. It found its mark between his eyes. The *ulua* bolted for the deep blue of the drop-off, the two spears poking like antennae from his brow.

It has been an easy, almost effortless dive day. The usually temperamental waters off O'ahu's Ka'ena Point were placid, seemingly beaten into laziness by the summer heat. The ocean here is full of fish, outrageous holes, and Hawai'ian myth and lore. I had paddled out on my longboard, which was also my diving platform, with two Hawai'ian sling spears, a mask, snorkel, fins, and a dive bag—all weighing no more than fifteen pounds, board included.

Within an hour the nine-foot-six-inch longboard was awash under sixty-five pounds of octopus, giant *uhu* (parrotfish), and a couple of seven-pound *kūmū* (highly prized goatfish). I was already headed in when I spotted my dream fish.

The *ulua* had put some distance between us despite the two spears stuck into him. I was three-quarters of a mile out and swimming with burning lungs and muscles against the current. My board had drifted downcurrent. It was a gamble to let it go and swim after the fish, but I couldn't afford to lose sight of my quarry for even a second.

The wobbling of the spears soon wore the *ulua* down enough so that I could use the best of my energy to surge ahead of him and herd him back toward the shallows. As my calves began to cramp, I was relieved to see the fish doing flips and violent spirals. He was dying.

Ulua are beautiful fish. They're smart, good hunters, and incredibly strong. I've seen them turn vicious when injured. As this *ulua* fluttered to a ledge thirty-five feet below, I realized that he didn't know that particular dead-end crevice as well as I did. It was the stroke of luck I needed to take a chance on retrieving my board. Three minutes later I was back with it, hovering over the crevice and relaxing my breathing to get a good gulp of air for the descent.

The *ulua* was scraping the spears against the ceiling of the ledge when I reached the opening. I sunk the fingers of one hand into his eye socket and

gripped the spear shaft protruding from his head with the other, and began to guide him out and up toward the surface.

He fought hardest two feet from the surface. My legs were starting to cramp and I was on the verge of blacking out. I shot out into the air, blasting the snorkel free of water, and for the first time felt the true heft of the fish. He felt like a lead umbrella.

As I wrestled the *ulua* up onto the deck of my board, I heard what sounded like wind blowing through reel lines or dogs barking. I pulled my mask off and followed the noise to a spot on the shoreline where four fishermen were jumping, yelling, and pointing at me. I grinned and raised the forty-five-pound trophy in a victory salute. Then, I turned my head back seaward just in time to see a fourteen-foot tiger shark barely fifty feet away, knifing toward my board, my sixty-five pounds of octopus and fish, my *ulua,* and my legs—not necessarily in that order.

A million heartbreaking thoughts and possibilities flashed into my mind, yet I had a solution to them all: Pulling myself into the less exposed knee-paddling position, I scuttled the *ulua* off the side, took a few pulls toward shore and said, "I'll be back . . . Next time catch your own dinner!" I didn't have the heart to do the "panic paddle" in, and so from a safe distance I watched my dream fish begin to sink. He wasn't even a foot under when the tiger grabbed him and tore into his midsection. My lungs, my arms, and the fishermen were screaming as I paddled away from the snapping, churning orgy.

Rell hanging five.

Big Rubber Pants

ON THE MORNING before our second date, the guy in question sent a fax to me at work saying he would be late for dinner but on time for *The Remains of the Day*. A sudden obligation to fish had arisen (along with mayflies on the Gunpowder), and he, along with several other government servants, could not let the country down. Something about the Clean Water Act and national security.

I worked in a newsroom at the time, a partitionless place where any attempt at privacy was considered an assault on the Constitution. The note was circulated long before I even knew of its existence, and its contents became the stuff of relentless in-house punditry. I was a single mother whose recent arrival from London had already made me a favorite topic of editorial opinion. A potential boyfriend had boosted my newsworthiness.

Consensus, though frequently hard to reach in my workplace, was that this man was a creative Lothario or the misogynous owner of camouflage garments. I betrayed no opinion one way or the other, but my heart had secretly soared at the mention of fishing. I longed to cast. I had seen my father, now long gone, try and try to catch a fish. He never looked happier, and he never reeled in a thing. "Does it get any better than this, Foo?" he'd say. I figured he ought to know. In between previews and the main feature that evening, I graciously forgave the Jujyfruit dinner and threw down a gauntlet. I asked my companion to teach me to fish. He said yes, shortly after Mr. Stevens said good-bye, forever, to Miss Kenton.

Several weeks later, a box arrived for me at work. By the time it got to my desk, a crowd had gathered. When I opened the package to reveal waders there was chaos. The object of my growing affection, crowed my angling-ignorant pals, clearly was a pervert and these "big rubber pants," as the photo editor called them, were a token of his sicko love. "Dump him," urged the political writer, "before he sends a whip and nipple rings."

It was so tempting to laugh, to take the advice of road-weary veterans and compose a witty rejection. Why leave the comfort of the pack and my favorite worst-case scenarios to be heartbroken, to be skunked again? Because why, snorted my inner child.

So I wore the pants. I learned to cast. I studied bugs. And I loved to fish. Hiking along the Gunpowder or the Potomac, eyeballing the water, stealing up to the bank and letting go. I hunted fish in my sleep; smelled the musty dank, gripped cork, leaned against the tugging cool around my knees. And woke up next to my guide and heartthrob. I loved him too—with caution.

That summer we fished one late afternoon on the middle fork of the Stanislaus River in California, our native habitat. The air was warm and still. The water was

Above: Jennifer Sweeney releasing a cut-throat, Yellowstone National Park.

Opposite: Casting.

ice-cold and moving fast, regrouping occasionally in deep pools, slowing at riffling turns—essentially a food-delivery system for some wild trout that were tantalizing in their proximity and confounding in their recognition of fraud. We crept and casted; hid and flicked line.

"Try another fly," suggested my swain. I took the fly box and found duns, mosquitoes, royal coachmen, and a diamond ring. I said yes before he could propose. He said yes too. We fished until dark, I scraped up the ring pretty bad, and he carried me over a swift-moving threshold to head home.

My colleagues bemoaned my need for the legal benediction of romance and begged me not to collect trout-themed tchotchkes. Behind my back, they collected for a silk teddy and started a pregnancy pool. And relegated my life to the sports section.

Paul Theroux

Traditional Time

TOWARD THE END of a long day paddling in the Trobriand Islands off the northeast coast of Papua New Guinea, I put ashore at a tiny seaside village, intending to ask permission to camp on a nearby beach. Stay here, the goggling villagers insisted. You will be safe. That also meant they could keep an eye on me. No one ever asked me how long I intended to remain in the village, though they were bewildered that I should prefer my tent to the hospitality of their huts. Fear of malaria— endemic and often fatal in the Trobriands—was my only reason. After two weeks of utter contentment, I paddled away.

They yelled, "Come back some time!"

A long time, months, passed before I returned, and when I did, without any warning, dragging my kayak out of the lagoon, a woman on the beach smiled at me and said, "We were just talking about you."

Her casual welcome delighted me. There was nothing remarkable about my reappearance; it was as though I had hardly left the village. I had thought of the intervening months as full of incident in my life. That same year was not a long time for them; it represented one harvest, and one storm, and several deaths. But no one truly dies in the Trobriands; they simply go to another island. The spirits of the dead reside on Tuma Island, just a bit north.

Their notion of the passage of time made my return less stressful. There was Trobriand protocol—ritual greetings and presents—but there was none of the drama and forced emotion that characterizes an American homecoming. It pleased me to think that I figured in their consciousness. Death or departure were part of an eternal return.

Such villagers are sometimes seen to be complacent. On the contrary, they are tenacious, secure, watchful, and patient. The Trobrianders are great voyagers be- cause they know how to bide their time. They wait weeks for the weather to break, and then set sail. And if they feel a storm is coming on they look for a rock or an atoll to find an anchorage. If the weather is bad, they hunker down. It doesn't matter if a trip takes days or weeks, it is the same voyage. The idea is to see it through to the end.

And the friendship of people who come and go for whatever length of time is not diminished by their absence. What matters in the Trobriands is your existence in the consciousness of the village. If someone talks about you, or if you appear in their dreams, you are present—you have reality.

"We've got to get this project finished!" aid workers yell. It is a Western notion of urgency to think in the bracketed term "time frame." But this suggests finite ef- fort, and limited funds, and perhaps limited goodwill. We Peace Corps volunteers

in Malawi used to wonder why the local bystanders smiled at us. They smiled at the odd belief that time is a fixed quantity; that time has a frame. In the societies on earth where there isn't much money, or it has little value, there are no limits to human effort or friendship or time. No one counts the hours required to make a canoe or a carving (which is why it is so easy for entrepreneurs to take advantage of people in such places). No one's departure is truly mourned, no one gets points for showing up again. This is also a metaphysical notion; people do not distinguish between the living and the dead, between what is mythical and what is real. The result is great harmony and immense patience.

In such a society, what is achieved matters much more than the simple passage of time. There is a Chinese parable quoted by Mao Tse-tung in which a man talks about moving a mountain—and he explains that it will be accomplished over generations. Perhaps this traditional sense of time, and its cosmology, is related to a short life span. It is not patronizing to say that there is a modesty and humility in Trobrianders and Malawians and people in rural China, whose lives are short. Nor is it fatalism on their part. The family, the clan, the village, the natural world— these are overwhelmingly more important in places where people expect to live only forty or fifty years. The phrase "a long time" is almost meaningless, and no one really dies and nothing really ends.

Fishing in Manado, Sulawesi.

Friendship

Kristine and Kate in Chile.

To Lola,

Shedding everything but our shirts to get across that river could be one of those moments when I am clearest about my good fortune of having a long-time friend. It's not so much the nonstop Patagonian wind blowing like crazy, kicking up that river to a froth. It's more the memory of us getting across it, hands clamped together, equally gripped by the situation we found ourselves in, and, finally, being out there, just the two of us, without our usual backup of husbands or boyfriends to figure it all out for us, their thirty years of experience in the extremes allowing us to follow along behind without that fear of drowningfalling-slidinggettingcaughtona—snag or any of the other number of quiet, dark thoughts we've had out there in the outthere.

No, we are at our best and closest when it is finally just the two of us, crawling across the pampas with packs far too heavy for our size because we couldn't leave behind journals, the black beans, and those creams we can't seem to live without. I take it as a good sign that some of our biggest laughs have come at our own expense.

When we are in our eighties and our sweethearts are older still, we will, finally, take them by the hand and show them what we know about the great outthere. Hah. We'll make sure they're safe.

With love and affection,
Birdy

Jack Turner

The Saddle

EACH YEAR AT THE END of our guiding season, I walk up to the Exum hut on the saddle between the Grand Teton and Middle Teton in order to bring down my climbing gear for the winter. I take it easy, loaf, and enjoy the solitude of autumn in the Tetons. This year the trip was different.

I left the Lupine Meadow parking lot in late afternoon under baleful skies. The cloud level hovered at eleven thousand feet and squalls were blowing through, carrying cold rain and sleet. I carried a light pack with two bottles of hot tea and a handful of Snickers bars.

By the time I reached the Meadows, two inches of snow covered the trail and things were looking a bit grim. Sheets of blowing snow veiled the lower walls of Nez Perce, the Middle Teton, and the ridges of Disappointment Peak. The summits disappeared into a pall of dark clouds as I put on gaiters and another fuzzy.

By the time I reached the Petzoldt Caves, snow concealed the trail. Two other guides were several hours in front of me, but I found their tracks only occasionally. Visibility was half a mile and diminishing rapidly. Everything is okay, I told myself, just a bit slower than usual. After all, I had probably walked up to the Saddle over three hundred times these past thirty-six years. But the light was fading and the world turning one color—the snow the soft gray of old pearls, the rocks a wet pewter. Above me I could hear the wind roaring through the towers on the south ridge of the Grand Teton.

The boulder field leading to the headwall was a mess—everything from cobbles to VW-size rocks covered with fresh snow. Visibility dropped to several hundred yards. The last steep stretch to the fixed rope was covered with crotch-deep snow the size of BBs. I was no longer climbing but wading.

Since I was not equipped to survive a night out, and no one knew where I was, my mind became a melee of images, most of them paranoid. I saw my body frozen like the Sioux at Wounded Knee. I began obsessing about who would find me, who would be called first.

The great poem by Hashin drifted through:
There is neither heaven nor earth,
Only snow
Falling, endlessly.

By the time I reached the fixed rope, it was dark and I was in a blizzard. When I turned on my headlamp, a cocoon of brilliant light, perhaps eight feet in diameter, enveloped me—thousands of scintillations from the blowing snow destroyed both my sense of place and direction. I turned it off, preferring the darkness with its vague but familiar forms.

On Mt. Teewinot, Tetons.

The fixed rope at the headwall was icy. I climbed, gripping it with my left hand, one foot on the rock, the other trying to stomp steps in a snow-filled chimney. The rock was greasy. In the summer this section is so easy we don't even belay clients, but on this dark night I was exhausted and off balance.

Then, in the darkness, without thought, my right hand searched the wall and brushed away snow. I sank my fingers into a great handhold. Yes. As I climbed on, I found more handholds, each buried under snow, each waiting for me like an old friend, each, I want to say, greeting me. Whoever knows a reef or river or mountain intimately knows, at some point, this feeling. It is among the gifts that flow from returning, again and again, each return enriching the cycle, forever. At another time and place, each of these handholds would have a name and I would greet them.

I felt calm. This was my home, these rocks, as much a home as I shall ever know.

Above the chimney, I set out at an angle toward the Saddle. I was wading again but no longer in a hurry. I stopped and drank tea. I downed a Snickers. Then I waded on, taking my time, relishing that lush privacy found only in great storms at night.

Suddenly, the wind grew stronger, the ground flat, and I knew I had arrived at the Saddle.

Light from a lantern glowed faintly through the Plexiglas door of the Exum hut.

I joined my fellow guides for dinner.

Ann Weiler Walka

Springwater

Snagged in shadow in Disappointment Valley, Colorado.

THE SANDSTONE RIM across the little river draws a dark edge on the silver sky as I crawl out of my sleeping bag to start the coffee water. My boots and sneaks still wet from yesterday's adventures, I pad barefoot down to the kitchen, an Ensolite pad under my arm. The sand is cold these early spring mornings, and I kneel on it while I pump the stoves. Moments after the hum ignites, sun transmutes the black rim to copper and my gaggle stirs, an occasional zipper further undoing the stillness. I always wince at folks rising into my own private morning, but especially on this trip with the overeager always-in-a-hurry travel writer and a trio of restless urbanites unable to settle into the just-greening-up, flood-debris-strewn canyon and always wanting to get "there."

My chores in hand, I hobble down the rocky trail to the river and choose the perfect place to splash my face, two sole-friendly river cobbles a heart's width apart and dry. Across the river, pink light unfurls above the chartreuse haze of willows; beneath, red roots curl from the undercut bank and drift on the purling water. A horse whinnies and the streaming, silty river wells with brilliant carmine and acid green, the glorious, supersaturated hues of a brand-new Technicolor world. Grinning, I splash my face with neon water. Good morning, morning. Up the bank the boy reporter stares dreamily at the swirling color and, beyond him, the woman who just yesterday blurted into the elegantly sexed throat of an evening primrose that she didn't care about flowers. Three of us lined up as motionless and attentive as herons along a fish-whispering eddy, morning flowing through us, all motion, all stillness.

Born again with numb feet and rose-colored eyeballs, an earful of the cheerful murmuring of birds, breath of willow and peppermint soap, and oh, the coffee. I head for the lime-laced cottonwoods, singing off-key. Bunched in a pool of sunshine, my goslings hold out their cups, beaming. On this third morning out we seem to have arrived.

Bungalow at Turneffe Flats, Belize.

Alice Waters

Cézanne's Carrot

The day is coming when a single carrot, freshly observed, will set off a revolution.
—Paul Cézanne

WE WERE IN a relatively remote spot on the Nayarit coast in Mexico, staying for a few days at a house the seven of us had rented together, uphill from a sunny, rocky beach. It was blazing hot. Most of us were cooks, and as cooks do when they are on vacation, we cooked. One of us, however, was a biochemist and an avid natural-ist, and he did as scientists might be presumed to do, by the same rule, on *their* vacations: He continued to do science. This he did, most notably, by freely sharing his knowledge—compulsively, gleefully, and captivatingly.

"Look!" he would cry—or whisper—and as we looked, his encyclopedic learn-ing would suddenly invest some newly seen phenomenon with a name, a context, and a story: He dove over and over into the surprisingly cold, rough water to gather specimens for an impromptu marine museum he set up on a stone wall in the sun, where he had us look through a magnifying glass at perfect little shells while he explained their underwater life cycles. In the mornings he rousted us to gaze at hundreds of pelicans flying to their feeding grounds, and at sunset one evening, he showed us spawning, sparkling little fish teeming in the surf. When we hiked to the village through the warm green shade of the jungle, he delivered brilliant dissertations on butterflies and ants. He helped us find barnacles and sea snails to gather for supper and could name every fish in the market. His enthu-siastic revelations of previously unimaginable other worlds transformed a lazy bus-man's holiday into a school of wonder.

To my shame, I have forgotten almost all the common names and simple facts I learned about the natural history of Nayarit and the Pacific Ocean, not to mention the phyla, genera, and species. But I cannot forget our friend's sharpened aware-ness, and it has occurred to me that we are fully human only when we bring such an exuberant acuity to all we do. On the question of how we are to eat, for ex-ample, it seems clear that if we make choices about food so as to bring us the most delight, we will also be protecting the environment and helping create communi-ties. When our senses are fine-tuned, the food that tastes best will be either wild or produced on a relatively small scale in such a way as to be a sustainable and envi-ronmentally sound occupation for generations. We can enjoy wild food when it has been hunted, fished, or gathered in ways that have produced no adverse envi-ronmental impact; and when we buy food that has been organically grown at local farmers' markets, we can enjoy food that is fresh and alive while supporting farmers who are truly taking care of the earth.

Jean Weiss

The Dress

THE DRESS IS BLACK, cocktail length, and not without flair. Its delicate lace bodice scoops lower in the back than in the front, revealing every bit of neck and shoulder one has to offer. With the slightest movement, the skirt's three chiffon tiers dally around each other like schoolgirls huddled in between chasing boys at recess. When I wear this dress, my hair pulled tightly back with a ribbon, I feel like a Spanish dancer.

Two miles of snow on a windswept road lie between me, my car, and the wearing of this dress at tonight's *Jackson Hole News* Christmas party. Today, as I figure how I'm going to get out, it seems cruel and unfair that the road into this Grand Teton National Park inholding has closed early my first season down here. It makes living alone in this small cabin just a little bit harder.

There are options to my party-dress dilemma, I know. I could ski out and borrow something else from a friend. I could carry out a pair of black slacks less likely to wrinkle. But for some reason, these are inadequate. It's the enormous abyss in my gut, not the desire to wear this dark dress, compelling me. Was my move to this lonely cabin rash? Was it smart to extract myself the way I did from a secure life with a handsome doctor? Had my joie de vivre survived the whole three-year ordeal? There it is, honestly and simply before me. I do not want to feel isolated in this cabin, in love, in wildness. I have to wear this dress tonight, wrinkle free and fully accessorized. With new resolve, I call the neighbors.

Yes, the caretakers of the ranch down the road respond; they are heading out in their Sno-Cat this morning. It is too early to send the dress and have it rumpled all day in my car, but I box up my high heels and coat and pile it into their Thiokol. The wildlife photographer who lives to the north snowmobiles out midday. Not a good ride for my dress either, but with him he carries my Secret Santa gift, a small box of jewelry, and a hair clasp.

Everything else out, there remains the dress. As the sun sinks behind the Tetons, shining light beams into my cabin through sections of broken shade, I pull on long underwear, layers of pile, and a hefty down jacket. I stretch skins over the base of my telemark skis, lace into leather boots, and find my gloves and poles.

It's cold tonight, maybe zero degrees. On my back is a pack containing a few toiletries, a change of clothes should I get stranded in town, and two pairs of stockings. Hooked to the top of my backpack on a hanger is the dress flowing freely in the wind. Enveloped in night halfway between my cabin and the road, I hear a gentle tapping as waves of chiffon delicately lap against me. Only the stars are loud—shimmering, applauding, and laughing around me, studding the sky like sequins, guiding me on.

Tetons.

136

Mark Wilford

Another Tricky Day

I WAS SOLOING about thirty feet above the Big Thompson River near Fort Collins in Colorado. The ice pillar I was on dripped due to the mild temperature, but that was normal for this time of year. The rubbery ice took my tool placements well, and below me the frozen river lay flat and clean. All in all, a mellow setting for ice bouldering.

Alas, it was not to last. I cranked up another move, pulled out the tool to make a placement, and crack! The pillar snapped. Completely detached, it accelerated downward at thirty-two feet per second squared, with me along for the ride. Then my remaining tool ripped out, freeing me from the pillar. I fell backward toward the ice below. The pillar plunged straight down, piercing the frozen river. As it drove into the ice, it displaced a layer of water over its surface. Into this three-inch skin of water I landed, flat on my back. It was just enough to break my fall. I jumped up and found the river's surface undulating under my feet: I was surfing a frozen wave. As I bolted for safety, I had to wonder, "Was that eight lives or nine?"

Above: Mark Wilford takes the big ride.

Opposite: Bridalveil Falls, Colorado.

Author Biographies

Carlos Andrade, a native of Kaua'i, is a musician, subsistence farmer/fisherman, and more recently, a grandfather and assistant professor at the Center for Hawai'ian Studies at the University of Hawai'i. He also sailed aboard *Hōkūle'a* from Rarotonga to Tahiti and Hawai'i in 1992. He keeps in touch with the ocean by surfing every chance he gets.

After many years of rambling around the Southwest as an environmental educator, wilderness instructor, park ranger, and journalist, **Ernest Atencio** recently returned to his 300-year-old northern New Mexico roots. He currently works for Amigos Bravos, a Taos, New Mexico–based river advocacy organization.

Rick Bass is the author of sixteen books of fiction and nonfiction, including a novel, *Where the Sea Used to Be.*

Dave Bean is a novelist and an essayist on National Pubic Radio. He lives and teaches at Gould Academy in Bethel, Maine, with his wife and daughter.

In 1985, **Eric Blehm** and his snowboard were shunned from almost every ski area in North America. He's been hiking, snowshoeing, and splitboarding for turns in the backcountry ever since—traveling the globe in search of powder, and writing articles for *Outside, Couloir, Snowboard Life, Powder,* and *TransWorld SNOWboarding,* where he was the editor for three years. He's currently writing and/or riding somewhere.

Tom Brokaw, award-winning anchor and managing editor of *NBC Nightly News,* has written articles and commentary for publications including the *New York Times, Newsweek, Life,* and *Outside.* His first book, *The Greatest Generation,* became a number-one bestseller after being published in 1998.

Paul Bruun came to Jackson, Wyoming, in 1973 to edit a local newspaper. Today, in addition to writing a weekly "Outdoors" *Jackson Hole News* column, he takes clients floatfishing on the Snake River during the summer and presents slide programs about fishing throughout the winter.

Susie Caldwell lives in an imitation Airstream trailer called *The Cyclone* in Santa Barbara, California. She finds solace in the mountains, on waves, and at the local donut shop.

Kitty Calhoun has climbed alpine routes throughout the United States, Alaska, South America, and the Himalayas. She enjoys playing with her son, Grady, and climbing as much as possible. She currently lives in Castle Valley, Utah, and works for High and Wild Mountain Guides.

Russell Chatham is a landscape painter and an author. He is also the founder and publisher of Clark City Press, and the proprietor of Chatham's Livingston Bar & Grill, a restaurant he designed and built in his hometown of Livingston, Montana.

Claire Chouinard, daughter of Yvon Chouinard, has been a Patagonia field tester since the day she was born. She is a farmer, poet, painter, and mother of four chickens. Claire is currently creating necessary mischief up and down the Pacific coast.

Yvon Chouinard is the founder of Patagonia, Inc. He started his career in the outdoor business as an itinerant surfer and climber selling handforged climbing gear from the back of his car. Since publishing his first one-page mimeographed catalog in 1964, he has built a company with a reputation for innovative design, durable quality, and a commitment to the environment.

Anthropologist **Wade Davis** received his Ph.D. in ethnobotany from Harvard, is author of seven books including his most recent, *Shadows in the Sun*, and has worked as a hunting guide, park ranger, and logger. He owns and runs a fishing lodge in British Columbia.

Michael Delp lives in northern Michigan. His most recent book is *The Coast of Nowhere: Meditation on Rivers, Lakes, and Streams.*

Daniel Duane is the author of *Caught Inside, A Surfer's Year on the California Coast,* and, most recently, *Looking for Mo.* He lives in San Francisco.

David James Duncan is the author of *River Teeth, The Brothers K,* and *The River Why.* He lives with sculptor Adrian Arleo and their family in Montana, where he is at work on a metaphysical comedy novel called *Letters from God.*

John Dutton lives and paddles in Santa Barbara, California. He races surfskis as well as solo and team outriggers. Surfing, sailing, and gardening provide alternative enjoyment.

Gretel Ehrlich, whose work has appeared in the *New York Times, Harper's, Time,* and *National Geographic,* is the author of twelve books. She divides her time between the Central Coast of California and northern Wyoming.

Larry Elsner lives in Austin, Texas, with his wife and daughter. He works in his family business and is board president of Austin Readers for School Libraries, an advocacy group for public school libraries.

Sam George is a professional surfer and has been writing about surfing for fifteen years. He is currently the field editor at *Surfer* magazine.

Accomplished rock and ice climber **Laurence Haston** shares her time between her Chamonix home and anywhere that's good for photography and experiencing the great outdoors. Favorite places include Nepal, northern Italy, and Spain. Favorite things include rock, ice, and really deep powder for snowboarding.

Formerly a stockbroker in Los Angeles, **Warren Hollinger** quit his career six months after being introduced to rock climbing. Warren settled in Salt Lake City with his lovely wife, Erika, and established himself as a premier professional climber, photojournalist, and public speaker. Warren's latest challenge has been recovering from a badly broken back sustained in a sixty-foot fall.

Sarah Malarkey is an editor at Chronicle Books in San Francisco.

Born in the urban confines of the East Coast in 1952, **Ron Matous** moved west after catching a glimpse of the Tetons during a summer climbing sojourn from the University of Connecticut. He has made a career of teaching and guiding in the mountains of Colorado and Wyoming as well as in Asia, South America, and elsewhere. He plans on living out his days in the shadow of the Grand Teton, where he has resided since 1977.

Bob McDougall was an expedition kayaker for eight years, traveling to such places as Russia, Pakistan, Ecuador, and Peru. Currently, he works as an aerial rigger for movies and commercials, lives in Ventura, California, and enjoys doing anything related to the water.

Born in Michigan, award-winning novelist **Thomas McGuane** is the author of such books as *The Bushwhacked Piano* and *An Outside Chance,* a collection of essays on sports. He is an ardent conservationist and lives with his family in McLeod, Montana.

Ellen Meloy is the author of *The Last Cheater's Waltz* and *Raven's Exile: A Season on the Green River.* She is a recipient of a Whiting Writer's Award. Her new book, *The*

Anthropology of Turquoise, is in progress. Meloy lives in southern Utah.

Dave Olsen is a former President and CEO of Patagonia. Before joining Patagonia, he led the development of solar, wind, hydro-, and geothermal power projects in more than twenty countries.

Dave Parmenter is well known in the surfing community as a surfer who writes rather than a writer who surfs. His work has appeared in a number of surfing magazines, including *Surfing, Surfer, Australian Surfing Life,* and *Surfer's Journal.* Dave splits his time between San Luis Obispo, California, and Makaha, Hawai'i.

Award-winning writer and cinematographer **Doug Peacock** spent twenty-five years studying grizzlies in Montana and Wyoming, and wrote about it in his book, *Grizzly Years: In Search of the American Wilderness.* The fictional character, Hayduke, in longtime friend Edward Abbey's *The Monkey Wrench Gang,* was based on Doug.

Mark Renneker is a forty-seven-year old surfer/physician specializing in case-specific patient advocacy and research, oncology, and surf medicine. He is an assistant clinical professor in the Department of

Family and Community Medicine, University of California, San Francisco, and founder of the Surfer's Medical Association.

Cameron Ridgeway, thirteen, lives with her family in Ojai, California. She loves to dance, play soccer, hike, climb, and ride horses, and would rather read a book than watch television any day.

Rick Ridgeway is a writer, photographer, and filmmaker. He is the author of four books, including *Seven Summits.* He is currently at work on his fifth, a story that begins on a remote peak in eastern Tibet—at the site of the avalanche that took the life of his close friend, and nearly his own. He lives with his wife and three children in Ojai, California.

As an outdoor writer, book author, and sports magazine editor, **Don Roberts** obsessively scours the watery recesses of the planet in search of fish and fish tales, but also something far more slippery: enlightenment. The scrapes and travails endured along the way keep his psychic compass fixed and the ink flowing.

Victor Saunders abandoned architecture to become a mountain guide. He now operates out of the French Alps and Himalayas.

David Scully pursues sailing, writing, engineering, and music in Charleston, South Carolina. He is president of Delta Marine Technologies, a business that designs and develops composite structures, including racing boats. He hopes to race around the world again . . . faster.

Lu Setnicka currently serves as Patagonia's Director of Public Affairs; she has been assistant to Yvon Chouinard and she worked four years as the Director of Recruitment. Prior to Patagonia, Lu spent many years working in national parks throughout North America: Yosemite, Everglades, the Grand Tetons, and Hawai'i Volcanoes. Lu has a degree in psychology from the University of California at Berkeley.

The mountains first became part of **Anne Smith**'s life while living in Chamonix, France, where she worked for Patagonia Europe and learned to climb. The mountains continue to play an integral role in her life as she learns to make her place among them in Colorado.

Jim Snyder has paddled white water since 1965 and was a prominent pioneer of squirt boating and steep creeking. He designs kayaks and makes handcrafted wooden paddles for a living.

John Sterling is Environmental Programs Associate at Patagonia. When not helping Patagonia support environmental organizations and issues, Sterling spends most of his time climbing and skiing in the Sierra Nevada backcountry.

The late Rell Sunn was one of the greatest all-around ocean athletes in Hawai'i since Duke Kahanamoku. She was called the "Queen of Makaha," and her regal grace was carried with her through a multifaceted career as a top professional surfer, Hawai'iana expert, radio personality, hula dancer, community leader, canoe racer, and expert free-diver.

Jennifer Foote Sweeney is a journalist who has worked for newspapers, a national news bureau, and at *Newsweek,* where she was deputy bureau chief in London. She is working as a mother at the moment, though she recently listed her occupation on a high school reunion questionnaire as "prima ballerina."

Author of fiction (most recently *Kowloon Tong*) and non-fiction (most recently *Sir Vidia's Shadow*), Paul Theroux has published thirty-five books and lives in Hawai'i.

Kristine McDivitt Tompkins worked at Patagonia for twenty-one years, serving as its CEO for fifteen years during her tenure. Today she remains on the Patagonia Board of Directors and resides in southern Chile with her husband, Douglas, managing their farms and 800,000 acres of their private native forest reserve.

Before Jack Turner turned to a more adventurous lifestyle, he taught philosophy at the University of Illinois. He has been climbing for the last thirty-six years in Colorado, Yosemite, and the Tetons, and has participated in over forty treks and expeditions to such places as India, Tibet, China, Peru, Nepal, and Pakistan. Turner divides his time between a remote ranch on the Mexican border during the winter, and Grand Teton National Park during the summer.

Itinerant grandmother, naturalist, and poet Ann Weiler Walka leads groups into the Colorado Plateau's backcountry during the outdoor season. In the winter, she explores landscapes on her own and with young writers. Ann authored *Waterlines: Journeys on a Desert River* and a forthcoming book about the Glen Canyon outback.

Alice Waters, internationally known chef, author, and proprietor of Chez Panisse restaurant—which is supplied by a network of local farmers who are committed to sustainable agriculture—pioneered the culinary philosophy based on using only the freshest ingredients, picked in season. Waters has also launched "The Edible Schoolyard," a curriculum that involves students in planting, harvesting, and cooking their own school lunches.

Jean Weiss, the senior features editor of *Women Outside,* lived in Jackson Hole, Wyoming, for nine years (the last three in the isolated cabin at the base of the Tetons) before moving to Boulder, Colorado. In Boulder, she's also worked as the executive editor of *Delicious!,* a natural lifestyle magazine, and as the senior editor of *Women's Sports & Fitness.*

Mark Wilford has been climbing for over twenty-five years. Climbing has taken him from the north face of the Eiger to the Himalayas. But his favorite area is still the sandstone boulders of his hometown in La Porte, Colorado.

With thanks to Drew Kampion, who thought of the first field reports.

With grateful thanks to Jane Sievert, Lorien Warner, and Amy Kumler.

Photo Credits